# *Sainthood Revisioned*

# Sainthood Revisioned

Studies in
HAGIOGRAPHY & BIOGRAPHY

Edited by Clyde Binfield

Sheffield Academic Press

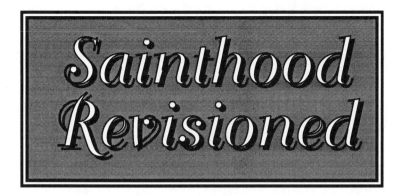

Published by
Sheffield Academic Press Ltd
Mansion House
19 Kingfield Road
Sheffield, S11 9AS
England

Typeset by Sheffield Academic Press
and
Printed on acid-free paper in Great Britain
by Bookcraft
Midsomer Norton, Somerset

British Library Cataloguing in Publication Data

A catalogue record for this book is available
from the British Library

ISBN 1-85075-289-3

CONTENTS

## Editor's Preface

For some years a Saturday seminar has met, once a term, in the University of Sheffield's Department of History. Its defining points have been morning coffee, lunch and afternoon tea (with cakes). Its theme, with variations, has been Religion and...: Religion and the Arts, Religion and Youth, Aggressive Religion, Religion and Unity, Religion and Politics, and so on. Religion has tended to be Christian although Islam, Buddhism and Confucianism have had their place and so, of course, has irreligion. Papers are offered rather than invited (unless the initial call is regarded as an invitation) and their delivery has varied in length from fifteen minutes to sixty. The size of the seminar too has varied, from five to twenty. Once the theme has been announced there is no attempt to tailor its components. This is because, call it serendipity or promiscuity, particular stimulus has been found in making connexions between the unlikeliest subjects. It is also because of the surprising discovery in what has traditionally been a self-consciously secular civic university that its history department's widest common denominator is the history of religion. At a time when research clusters are modish and centres, schools and institutes are all the rage, historians, who are notoriously independent people, are vulnerable. When history was first taught in the University of Sheffield those who taught it were expected to teach everything. Now they merely have to teach everybody, but their teaching seldom goes beyond their research expertise and that has become steadily more specific. The generalist is an endangered species. Hence the stimulus of a day in which a paper on Byzantium or the Celtic Church can stand alongside one on Congregationalism in Purley between the Wars or religion in Japan, or (as in the present case) when Comenius, Defoe and Rousseau can consort with St Patrick, Sir Oswald Mosley (as seen by A.K. Chesterton) and the manufacturer of Chivers jam. For these papers were delivered at such a seminar. They are essays in doing history regardless of current fashion.

Clyde Binfield

## List of Contributors

CLYDE BINFIELD is Reader in History at the University of Sheffield and was head of its Department of History from 1988 to 1991. He has written on the history of the English YMCAs and of the World Alliance of YMCA as well as on the social and cultural aspects of English Nonconformity. He chaired the editorial board of the *History of the City of Sheffield 1843–1993* (Sheffield Academic Press, 3 vols., 1993), contributing the section on 'Religion in Sheffield', and he is to contribute a volume on Christianity in Britain between 1789 and 1914 to the *Oxford History of the Christian Church*.

MICHAEL BOOTH FRSA teaches in Helmsley and taught in Histon. He is a graduate of the college of Ripon and York St John, the University of Leeds and the University of Sheffield, where he worked on 'Parish and Gathered Church: A Comparison of Evangelical Protestantism in South Yorkshire and Cambridgeshire, 1789–1914'.

JAMES HUNTLEY GRAYSON is Senior Lecturer in Modern Korean Studies and Director of the Centre for Korean Studies at the University of Sheffield. He is an anthropologist who has written *Korea: A Religious History* (Oxford University Press, 1989) and is now engaged in a comparative study of the foundation myths of Korea and other Northeast Asian societies.

LINDA KIRK lectures in the Department of History at the University of Sheffield. A historian of the Enlightenment, she is the biographer of Richard Cumberland and is preparing a history of Geneva in the eighteenth century.

JAN KUMPERA teaches history at the University of West Bohemia, Plzen, where he has served as Vice-Rector. An authority on Comenius, he was a visiting Fellow in the Department of History at the University of Sheffield while working on the University's Hartlib Project.

ANDREW MITCHELL teaches history and politics at Basingstoke College. He is working on Fascism in East Anglia in the 1930s.

PHILIP MULREANY teaches at the London Management Centre, University of Westminster. He is working on North London's Dissenting communities and entrepreneurship between 1660 and 1850.

JANE STEVENSON is Lecturer in History at the University of Sheffield, where her fields are late antiquity and early medieval history. Her publications include the second edition of *The Liturgy and Ritual of the Celtic Church* and articles on Latin literature, Byzantine sports and politics and the early history of literacy in Ireland.

GARTH TURNER is Rector of Tattenhall and Handley, Cheshire. He has written on Dean Hussey of Chichester and is working on the Anglican clergy of Victorian Derbyshire.

## Introduction

*Clyde Binfield*

These nine studies have the University of Sheffield's Department of History in common. That is to say, they were all papers delivered in the Department by scholars who are, or hope to be, graduates of the University, or who teach or have taught in it, or who have been associated with it for some time. In this way universities in the Czech Republic and London are associated with Sheffield. Their subjects range geographically from the British Isles to Bohemia and on to Manchuria and Korea, and chronologically from early medieval Ireland to England in the later twentieth century. They embrace saints, bishops, philosophers, demagogues, Baptists and Wesleyan Methodists and those who embrace them include an economic historian, a social historian, an anthropologist and a historian of thought as well as ecclesiastical historians.

It is the anthropologist in the group, James Grayson, who sensibly turns first to dictionary definitions: hagiography is 'the writing of the lives of saints' (*Oxford English Dictionary*) or 'venerated persons' (*Merriam-Webster*); a hagiography can also be an 'idealizing or idolizing biography' (*Merriam-Webster*). The relationship between them is thus as obvious as it is obviously uneasy.

We begin literally with hagiography, with early Irish saints. Jane Stevenson reconsiders the three most famous, Bridget, Columba and Patrick. It goes without saying that their *Lives*, like their lives, are not what they seem. For their first treatment, 200 years after the event, was in a mode quite divorced from most understandings of history or biography. Hagiography is about sanctity. The sanctity of Bridget (if she ever existed), of Columba (that 'redeployed dynast') and of Patrick (that doubly handicapped 'dubious...Romano-British *episcopus vagans*') was only relevant if it could be popularized as power. Hence Dr Stevenson's study, ranging from Ireland through Iona to Northumbria, is an essay in the politics of power.

Politics is the link with Comenius, the first of three figures in this collection who encompass the European Enlightenment. To study Comenius is to study a man who is constantly being forgotten and as constantly resuscitated. It is also to study the politics of inspired pedagogy. And it is also about the religious world of Bohemian (and West European) Reformers and the more secular world of Czech nationalism. Jan Kumpera surveys the consequently shifting image of Comenius. When Professor Kumpera delivered his paper Comenius studies were rapidly emerging from their Communist carapace. The Comenius who appealed to Czechoslovakia's three democratic presidents (Masaryk, Beneš and Havel) had become the man to watch. Now that Comenius too will be redefined to fit the nationalism of two republics, the Czech and the Slovak.

Pedagogy and dissent within the Reformed tradition provide the link with Philip Mulreany's essay on Defoe and Linda Kirk's on Rousseau. Each, if not canonized, has most certainly fostered a canon. Of Defoe's relationship to English Protestant Dissent there can be no doubt, but what that relationship was is a matter of considerable doubt. Like any inspired journalist and publicist Daniel Defoe has been God's gift to the pigeon-holing generalist. Defoe, the social observer, has fired a fine succession of economic historians. Lettrists have been stimulated by Defoe's Dissenting context and Dissenters have taken pride in it. Mr Mulreany queries all of it. His Defoe is both myth and myth-maker. Nonetheless any study of Defoe must still be an essay in the politics of dissent (even of Dissent) and Mulreany confirms, at least implicitly, one prime fact about the English Dissenting world: though it was increasingly a ghetto world, diminishing and turning in upon itself, it yet retained the mentality of a mainstream alternative. Its concern with order, not least the complex of relationships depending on its understanding of church order, is testimony to that. Neither in their education nor in their religious observance did Dissenters suddenly leap ahead of their times or find themselves sidelined. And since they were never entirely excluded from public life their inevitable ambivalence becomes understandable. In this regard Defoe, whose ambivalence is the motor of Mr Mulreany's essay, remains a Dissenter writ unrepresentatively large.

Jean-Jacques Rousseau comes to mind even less than Daniel Defoe as a product of Reformed Protestantism. Yet Geneva was more his city than it was Calvin's, since at least Rousseau was born there. With clear-eyed naughtiness Linda Kirk reflects on, perhaps 'reconstructs' would be a better word, the relationship between that city and one of its most famous citizens. Certainly here are displayed all the elements of goodness, as defined in the Beatitudes and as understood by any Reformed congregation of saints, and here are considered their tiresome implications for a Reformed body politic in the Enlightenment's high noon.

The nineteenth century was hagiology's high noon. All sorts of men and women were candidates for treatment. Here we have three approaches to some candidates. Michael Booth considers Stephen Chivers the jam maker, a man after Samuel Smiles's heart. Chivers displays all the currently deprecated elements of paternalism if not patriarchy and the surviving written evidence reinforces the image. What needs to be disinterred, however, is the consistency in the family witness (at least four Baptist generations) and the now forgotten emphasis that these apparently autocratic strivers after community placed on simple *usefulness*. Whatever their ambition, part of that ambition was to be useful.

Such usefulness is surely one clue to an understanding of John Ross, whose biographer, James Grayson, is the only contributor to admit to hagiography. It may be that in thus commemorating Manchuria's pioneer Protestant missionary (not least through the perspectives of his own missionary experience in Korea) Dr Grayson is achieving for that mission what in past centuries was achieved for the Jesuit missions to China and Japan or, more mythical by far, for St Thomas and those who followed him in India.

Stephen Chivers's spirituality was formed in Wesleyan

Methodism but it was, it seems, accented by his Baptist wife. Clyde Binfield explores the role of women in transmitting the faith. He selects a group of middle-class Wesleyan women. Their spirituality is couched conventionally, much of it self-consciously, as if they were preparing notes for the funeral sermons that would summate their sojourn in this vale of tears. It has resurfaced at a time when women's studies are greedy for such material, though they are least likely to place the emphasis where these women would have placed it: in the household of faith.

So to what might appear to be the cuckoo in the nest, Andrew Mitchell's study of Oswald Mosley as seen by A.K. Chesterton. Here, certainly, is an essay in the politics of power and the rhetoric of sanctity even if Mosley is not to be hagiographed into a Columba or a Patrick (and Cynthia and Diana are no Bridgets). The context is significant here. The Mosleys were landed gentry who had been greatly helped by real estate and manorial rights in Manchester. The Chesterton money came from successful estate agency in London. A.K. Chesterton's relationship to Oswald Mosley was thus an unusually apt one. Few landed families were without a strong clerical infusion; and A.K. Chesterton's rhetoric is the mirror image of his famous kinsman's:[1]

> Tie in a living tether
> The prince and priest and thrall
> Bind all our lives together,
> Smite us and save us all;
> In ire and exultation
> Aflame with faith, and free,
> Lift up a single nation
> A single sword to thee.

That G.K. Chesterton hymn, in current hymn books[2] and still sometimes sung by venturesome congregations, might introduce

1. Arthur Kenneth Chesterton (1899–1973) and Gilbert Keith Chesterton (1874–1936) were second cousins.

2. 'O God of earth and altar' (tune: King's Lynn) is thus 578 in *Congregational Praise* (London: *Independent Press*, 1951); 426 in *Hymns and Psalms* (London: Methodist Publishing House, 1983); and 346 in *Rejoice and Sing* (Oxford: Oxford University Press, 1991).

Garth Turner's essay on episcopal biography since the Second World War. Here are few saints, either as subjects or authors, though here is great material for ample biography by no means liberated from the strategies and presuppositions which shaped, for instance, the first lives of those early Irish saints. Even so, on the evidence here, one hopes that episcopal biography will live on, though clerical biography is not what it was, the market being what it is.

## Early Irish Saints: Some Uses of Hagiography

*Jane Stevenson*

The hagiography of early medieval Ireland curiously resembles a race in which there are three favourites and the rest of the field is nowhere. When the great Jesuit scholar Father John Colgan, in the seventeenth century, collected together the hagiography relating to early Ireland, he created two large folio volumes of approximately equal size. One is called *Acta Sanctorum Hiberniae*,[1] the other is known as *Trias Thaumaturga*[2] and contains the dossiers relating to Ireland's three most significant saints.

Ireland's three thaumaturges are a very peculiar group indeed. The first was a dubious fifth-century Romano-British *episcopus vagans*, labouring under two main handicaps: the suspicion and distrust of his immediate superiors, and the fact that he was not Irish, therefore a person who could not own land, and subject to the arbitrary whims of Ireland's rulers.[3] The second was almost certainly a superannuated goddess;[4] a

1. Louvain, 1645.

2. In full, *Triadis Thaumaturgae, seu divorum Patricii Columbae et Brigidae, trium veteris et maioris Scotiae, seu Hiberniae, sanctorum insulae, communium patronorum acta* (Louvain, 1647).

3. Technically, *cu glas*: a person without status or honour-price. In Irish, as to some extent in Germanic, law, the rights of the individual were directly dependent on his position within a family. See C. Stancliffe, 'Kings and conversion', *Frühmittelalterliche Studien* 14 (1980), p. 64.

4. The goddess Brigantina is well attested in Roman-Celtic Britain (see Anne Ross, *Pagan Celtic Britain* [London, 1967], pp. 160-62): she is of course the patroness of the Brigantes of Yorkshire (Brythonic **Briganti*). Brigit is the Irish reflex of the same name. Later in medieval Ireland, there is mention of a triple goddess named Brigit. The name is very ancient: the

personage with no identifiable historical reality whatsoever. The third was a redeployed dynast from the most ambitious and bloody-minded family in sixth-century Ireland, considerably handicapped by his having been excommunicated by a general synod of Irish ecclesiastics. The three, of course, are Patrick, Brigit, and Columba.[5]

It should be clear that as founding saints, all three were problematic.[6] It is perhaps for this very reason that their seventh-century successors were the first Irishmen to grasp the significance of written propaganda as a tool for power and advancement.[7] The beginnings of Irish and Hiberno-Latin literature are datable to the end of the seventh century, and mostly associable with a small number of major religious foundations. It has been memorably said that the Uí Néill (Columba's family) emerge into history 'like a school of cuttlefish, in a cloud of ink of their own manufacture'.[8] The same may be said of Armagh, Kildare and Iona. There were three lives of St Brigit by the end of the seventh century, one in Old Irish, two in Latin, the first dating to *circa* 630; two lives of St Patrick, written around 630–650, preserved with additional material relating to that saint of Armagh; and last, a life of Columba written by Adomnán, his

Celtic root *brgnti* is paralleled by Sanskrit *brhati*: 'the (female) exalted one'.

5. The Hiberno-Latin lives of Brigit are edited by Colgan, and also in the Bollandist's *Acta Sanctorum*, 2 February. The Old Irish *Bethu Brigte* is edited by D. O hAodha (Dublin, 1978). St Patrick's dossier is in *The Patrician Texts in the Book of Armagh* (ed. L. Bieler; Dublin, 1979). The most recent edition of Adomnán is *Adomnán's Life of Columba* (ed. A.O. and M.O. Anderson; Edinburgh, 1961).

6. It may here be added that there is no fifth-century evidence to connect Patrick with Armagh at all; and since it was without doubt an important pre-Christian religious site, Richard Sharpe has suggested that the earliest cult of St Patrick, like that of St Brigit, was the initiative of a converted druidic college finding itself in need of a patron ('St Patrick and the See of Armagh', *Cambridge Medieval Celtic Studies* 4 [1982], pp. 55-56).

7. See further J. Stevenson, 'Hiberno-Latin literacy: the evidence of the Patrick dossier in the Book of Armagh', in *The Uses of Literacy in Early Medieval Europe* (ed. R. McKitterick; Cambridge, 1990), and J.-M. Picard, 'The purpose of Adomnán's *Vita Columbae*', *Peritia* 1 (1982), pp. 161-64.

8. J.V. Kelleher, 'Early Irish history and pseudo-history', *Studia Historica* 3 (1963), pp. 113-27.

kinsman and ninth successor as abbot (or *comarba*: 'heir') of Iona, in the 680s.

These lives are interconnected in various ways, particularly the lives of Brigit and Patrick.[9] Muirchu begins his life of Patrick with an elaborate extended metaphor concerning 'this deep and perilous sea of sacred narrative', 'on which so far no boat has ventured except the one of my [spiritual] father Coguitosus'. He evidently refers to the life of Brigit by Cogitosus of Kildare. Furthermore, both Muirchú and his contemporary at Armagh, Tírechán, used 'a book in the possession of Ultán, bishop of Connor', also referred to as *plana historia*: 'a straightforward history', containing information about St Patrick of, it seems, remarkably diverse kinds, including an Old Irish poem, and a lost Hiberno-Latin hymn.[10] Ultán is also known to have made a collection of material relating to Brigit, which was used at Kildare,[11] and thus seems to have been something of a specialist in hagiography. The interconnectedness of Armagh, in the North, and Kildare, in the South, at a literary, scholarly, and personal level is also matched by their political relationship. The Armagh 'Book of the Angel' from the Patrick dossier, ends:

> Between holy Patrick and Brigit, pillars of the Irish, there existed so great a friendship of charity that they were of one heart and one mind...The holy man, then, said to the Christian virgin: 'O my Brigit, your *paruchia* [roughly, area of political influence] will be deemed to be in your province in your dominion [*monarchia*], but in the eastern and western part it will be in my domination.'

Brigit has borne the title of 'Queen of the South' from that day to this. What we can see quite clearly here is that Armagh and Kildare in the later seventh century have agreed to support

9. Though Adomnán of Iona probably read the life of Brigit by Cogitosus: see D.A. Bullough, 'Columba, Adomnán and the achievement of Iona', *Scottish Historical Review* 43 (1964), pp. 111-30; 44 (1965), pp. 17-33, esp. 44, pp. 19-21. Iona was certainly aware of the importance of Armagh and vice versa, since Tírechán can be seen to be fighting back against competition from Iona (*Patrician Texts, Additamenta* 18[1], 22[1], pp. 138, 140). In addition, Adomnán refers to one 'Maucteus, discipulus Patricii', showing that he knew of Patrick's existence.

10. J. Stevenson, 'The beginnings of literacy in Ireland', *Proceedings of the Royal Irish Academy* 89 C (1989), p. 154.

11. R. Sharpe, '*Vitae S. Brigidae*: the oldest texts', *Peritia* 1 (1982), pp. 99-100.

rather than to undermine each other. Brigit's claim to hegemony is comprehended within Patrick's larger claim, but it is recognized.

If Armagh and Kildare had parcelled Ireland out between them by 650, how was the third thaumaturge to establish himself? The answer is obvious. Northern Ireland, the Uí Néill homeland, had been spilling over on to the west coast of Scotland for generations before the birth of Columba. By the end of the sixth century, Argyll was Irish-speaking, displacing the Northern branch of the Britons southwards into what became Cumbria, and pushing the Picts north and eastwards. Columba followed this movement, setting up his chief monastery at Iona, off Mull, and became, *par excellence*, not just the Uí Néill's family saint, but the saint of Gaelic Scotland. When Cinaed (Kenneth) mac Alpin unified Scotland under an Irish king in the ninth century, Columba was his patron. The kings of Scotland were buried in Columban centres, Iona and later, Dunkeld, for centuries. Thus the youngest of the trio did not so much seek to compete with the other two, as to open up new ground.

The life of Columba is unique in early Irish hagiography. Columba died in 597, and Adomnán wrote some eighty years later; thus, Adomnán's life was written within living memory of its subject. He names his sources in his preface, scrupulously:

> I shall relate what has come to my knowledge through the tradition passed on by our predecessors, and by trustworthy men who knew the facts...either from among those things that we have been able to find put into writing before our time, or else from among those we have learned, after diligent enquiry, by hearing them from the lips of certain informed and trustworthy aged men who related them without any hesitation.

A recent survey of Adomnán's sources and methods has amply confirmed the truth of this assertion of scholarly method.[12]

The reason why Adomnán's life of Columba has this historical character may perhaps be sought in his scholarly milieu. Although he was certainly in touch with Ireland, he was also in touch with Northumbria, whose centre of evangelization, at

12. M. Herbert, *Iona, Kells and Derry: The History and Hagiography of the Monastic Familia of Columba* (Oxford, 1989), pp. 12-26.

Lindisfarne, was manned from Iona, and which happened at this time to be undergoing something of a golden age of historiography.[13] Apart from the towering achievement of Bede, the floresence of late-seventh-century Northumbrian culture produced the Lindisfarne life of Cuthbert, which incidentally shares a whole clutch of literary borrowings with Adomnán's life of Columba,[14] a life of archbishop Wilfred, a life of the abbots of Wearmouth, and a life of Gregory the Great. Adomnán, personally known to Bede, and a friend of the scholarly, half-Irish Northumbrian king, Aldfrith, seems to have been influenced in the composition of his great work by the Northumbrian tradition.

It must be emphasized that the rest of early Irish hagiography is entirely different. The date of Patrick's death is a subject of considerable controversy, but it must have occurred at some point in the fifth century. We may thus say that the Armagh lives were written some two hundred years after their subject's death. Brigit is placed by those lives that secure her in time at all as contemporary with Patrick, thus, in the fifth century.

This is the normal state of affairs with Irish hagiography. No saint has a contemporary biographer. The monastic houses of Ireland, striving in vain to catch up with the lead given them by Armagh and Kildare, exploded into a flurry of hagiographic activity from the eighth century onwards. These saints' lives relate to the founders of monasteries, Ciaran of Clonmacnoise, Caoimhin of Glendalough, Brendan of Birr, Comgall of Bangor, and many others. It is due to this frenzied activity in monastic scriptoria the length and breadth of Ireland that the sixth century subsequently acquired the title of 'the age of the saints'. But again, the writing of the lives post-dates the living of them by two hundred years. There were great men in the Irish church of the eighth and ninth centuries, notably the formidable Máel Ruain of Tallagh, Ireland's equivalent to Benedict of Aniane as a founder and reformer of monasteries. Though his achievement was clearly remarkable, he attracted no biographic attention whatsoever. This suggests that, leaving Adomnán to

13. For a survey of this see W. Goffart, *Narrators of Barbarian History (AD 550–800)* (Princeton, New Jersey, 1988), pp. 235-320.

14. Bullough, 'Columba, Adomnán and the achievement of Iona', pp. 129-30.

one side as a special case, the Irish concept of hagiography had no connection with the idea of history whatsoever.[15] Instead, the concept of 'the age of the saints'—that is, that about 90 per cent of Irish people culted in Ireland flourished in the sixth century—and the consequent refusal of sanctity to persons who were historically accessible, pulls early Irish hagiography out of the realms of biography entirely, and turns it into something quite different.

We must then ask what an early Irish saint's life was *for*. It was a highly abstract genre, and the preoccupations which emerge repeatedly from the texture of the writing itself are power, status, and the expression of seventh-century political relationships.

The property dimension emerges most nakedly in the *additamenta* to Tírechán's life of Patrick, which effectively form a sort of narrative cartulary. For instance:

> Binén macc Lugu...was the son of a daughter of Lugath macc Netach. His mother's kin gave him his hereditary land, on which he founded a church, consecrated to God and offered to Patrick, and holy Patrick marked the place for himself with his staff, and he was the first to offer there the body and blood of Christ.

This passage confirms first, Binen's legal right to alienate this territory, second, Patrick's claim on it. Another example is still more blatant:

> Patrick came to the territory of Calrige and baptized Macc Cairthin and Caíchán, and after he had baptized them, Macc Cairthin and Caíchán offered to God and Patrick the fifth part of Caíchán's estate, and the king exempted it for God and Patrick. These are the boundaries of the fifth part, that is, Caíchán's fifth: From the stream of Telach Berich out of Braidne as far as...Tuilgos from the mountain. From the Stream of Conaclid to Reiri and from the border of Druimm Nit to the stream of Tamlacht Dublocho, and the stream to Grenlach Fote. Along Ront round...to the Moor of the Two Hillocks...and so on and so on, all round the boundary.[16]

15. For specific examples, see for instance R. Sharpe, '*Quatuor sanctissimi episcopi*: Irish saints before St Patrick', in *Sages, Saints and Storytellers: Celtic Studies in Honour of Professor James Carney* (Maynooth, 1989), pp. 376-99.

16. 8 (1), Bieler (ed.), *Patrician Texts*, p. 173.

This is an entirely legalistic passage of prose, designed solely to establish Patrick's unencumbered possession of a very specific tract of territory. 'The Book of the Angel' tells the same story, though in a more inclusive and imprecise fashion:

> Every free church and city of episcopal rank which is seen to have been founded in the whole island of the Irish, [is]...in special union with bishop Patrick, and the heir of his see of Armagh, because, as we have said above, God has given him the entire island.[17]

It should perhaps be stressed that the name 'Patrick' in a hagiographical context *always* means the ahistorical, eternal Patrick—which is to say, for all practical purposes, his heir in direct line of succession at Armagh, his *coarb*, in Old Irish. The alleged giving of a church to 'Patrick' by the fifth-century individual Binen conveys, or is intended to convey, a living reality relating to the land-holdings of mid-seventh-century Armagh.

The lives are also used to convey the power and political clout of their heroes—which, again, implies the status that their coarbs should be accorded by others. In Adomnán's life of Columba, the position of respect Columba enjoyed among his fellow monastic founders is heavily underlined, for instance in the following passage:

> At another time, four holy founders of monasteries crossed over from Ireland to visit Saint Columba...the names of these illustrious men were Comgell mocu-Aridi, Cainnech mocu-Dalon, Brenden mocu-Alti, Cormac grandson of Lethan. They chose, all with one accord, that Saint Columba should consecrate the sacred mysteries of the Eucharist in the church, in their presence.[18]

Thus, his successor and heir presents him as *primus inter pares*, despite the handicap of having once been excommunicated. Monastic founders were abbots and priests, not bishops, and the normal custom when no bishop was present was for priests to concelebrate. Thus the honour here paid to Columba by his fellow-abbots is marked. Another passage in the same work emphasizes Columba's significance in secular politics:

17. 23, Bieler (ed.), *Patrician Texts*, p. 189.
18. III, 17, Anderson and Anderson, *Life of Columba*, p. 501.

> The holy man…sailed over to the island of Io [Iona], and there, as he had been bidden [by an angel] he ordained as king Aidan, who arrived about that time. And among the words of the ordination he prophesied future things of Aidan's sons, and grandsons, and greatgrandsons. And laying his hand upon Aidan's head he ordained and blessed him.[19]

This passage is the earliest reference to ecclesiastical intervention in the investiture of a king anywhere in Europe, and has consequently generated an enormous amount of controversy. The immediate focus of interest for this paper is not so much in the precise liturgical implications of Adomnán's imprecise words, as in the fact that Aidan mac Gabran was a very important and powerful king of Scottish Dalriada (in which Iona was geographically situated), and that his grandchildren and great-grandchildren were powers in the land at the time when Adomnán was writing. For Adomnán to underline that Columba stands in relation to the line of Aidan roughly where the prophet Samuel stood in relation to the house of David has obvious implications for the respect in which his great-grandsons ought to hold the abbot of Iona. The Old Testament resonances of Adomnán's prose are underscored in a different passage of the life, when Aidan allegedly asked Columba which of his three sons would succeed him.

> The saint then spoke in this manner: 'None of these three will be king, for they will fall in battles, slain by enemies. But now, if you have others that are younger, let them come to me, and the one whom the lord has chosen from among them to be king will run at once to my knee.'

He did, of course: Columba's second sight, or Adomnán's hindsight? Either way, his intimate relationship with both God and the leading dynasty of Dalriada is strengthened and buttressed by all such assertions.

The principal contents of seventh-century Irish saints' lives can often be related directly to a Darwinian struggle for the survival of the fittest. Ireland has never been a wealthy country, and only a proportion of its wealth and resources could reasonably go to the Church. The question was then, of

19. III, 5, Anderson and Anderson, *Life of Columba*, p. 475.

course, which churches? which monasteries? By and large, each dynasty had its own saint, its own foundation, on a principle resembling the Continental *eigenkloster*, and they rose and fell together: thus Bangor, the monastery of St Comgall, was one of the five most intellectually significant monasteries in seventh-century Ireland, and allegedly housed something like two thousand monks, but by the mid-eighth century, the displacement of its patrons, the rulers of Irish Dalriada, by the Uí Néill, caused it to have dwindled into complete insignificance long before the Vikings finished it off for good. Competition for resources between different houses was savage. The winners, Armagh, Iona and Kildare, were the ones who contrived not only to attach a powerful and rising local dynasty, but also to extend their influence across the whole of the Irish world. It is no accident that the first named person to create a new law and get it accepted across the whole of Ireland was not a king, even of the Uí Néill, but Adomnán of Iona.[20] The second such law was 'the law of Patrick'.[21] Very clearly, the saints' lives, as propaganda for the power and influence of their subjects, had a crucial role to play in aggrandizing specific monastic centres at (inevitably) the expense of others.

Another aspect of these lives which is noteworthy and distinctive is the idea of sanctity that they embody. The detachment of the saint from any concept of common humanity is most clearly seen in Patrick, where the inventions of his hagiographers can actually be contrasted with his own autobiographical writing, his *Confessio* and *Epistola ad Coroticum*. Patrick's human personality comes over very clearly; a man desperately in earnest, possessed by the vision of his faith, in and out of

20. It protected women's status as non-combatants, and the codification was signed by more than forty Irish kings and forty leading churchmen, starting with the coarb of Patrick, from all over Ireland. Anyone who violated the law had to pay a fine to Iona. See M. Ní Donnchadha, 'The guarantor list of *Cáin Adomnáin*, 697', *Peritia* 1 (1982), pp. 193-94. It was not the first of the *cánai*: the earliest known example is *Cáin Fhuithirbe*, datable to the 670s or 680s (edited and translated in L. Breatnach, 'The ecclesiastical element in the Old-Irish legal tract *Cáin Fhuithirbe*', *Peritia* 5 [1986], pp. 36-52, dating criteria pp. 45-47).

21. It protected the non-combatant status of clerics: a clear case of copycat legislation.

prison, in daily fear of martyrdom, labouring under suspicion of financial mismanagement, ill-educated, and trusting blindly to his sense of mission. He is truly heroic in his very defensiveness and weakness, in the courage with which he faced his expectation of violent death. When his converts were carried off as slaves by the pagan ruler Coroticus, the outraged Patrick's sole resource was to excommunicate him; a sanction which Coroticus is unlikely to have respected in the spirit in which it was intended.

This remarkable person was not what Muirchú and Tírechán needed as a hero. Patrick's writings were known and read at Armagh, but clearly, they would not do at all. Muirchú's Patrick is a shining lamp of the holy spirit, kings grovel at his feet, he tramples on druids and all their works, cursing, banning, bringing people back from the dead. Divine wrath instantly comes to his aid. This is what Muirchú does with the real Patrick's impotent wrath, expressed in his jeremiad to Coroticus:

> News had been brought to him of a wicked act by a certain British king named Corictic, an ill-natured and cruel ruler...Patrick tried to call him back to the way of truth by a letter, but he scorned his salutary exhortations. When this was reported to Patrick, he prayed to the Lord and said: 'My God, if it is possible, expel this godless man from this world and from the next'. Not much time had elapsed after this when [Corictic] heard somebody recite a poem saying that he should abandon his royal seat, and all the men who were dearest to him chimed in. Suddenly before their eyes, in the middle of a public place, he was ignominously changed into a fox, sent off, and since that day and hour, like water that flows away, was never seen again.[22]

This is what early medieval Ireland expected. A saint should be a mighty curser, a tireless ascetic, a wonderworker, a prophet and seer, and an indefatigable guardian of his rights, lands and treasures. He should not be a mere mortal, transcending the limits of the human condition by sheer force of will. Thus, the powerful drive to project a fantasy of power on to the concept of sanctity meant that, in practice, the only good saint was one who had been dead long enough to have been completely forgotten.

22. I, 29, Bieler (ed.), *Patrician Texts*, p. 101.

# Comenius: Between Hagiography and Historiography. Reflections on the Changing Image of the Czech Reformer

*Jan Kumpera*

Few personalities in Czech and European cultural history have undergone so many changes of image as Johannes Amos Comenius (Jan Amos Komensky). His European reputation achieved its first peak during his life, although his language textbooks were generally more accepted and more widely published than his reform proposals and treatises. He became during his own lifetime a respected and distinguished educationalist, despite the fact that he considered himself—maybe a little self-confidently—a universal reformer of human affairs.

In Comenius's view education should be more comprehensive, more democratic, more practical and useful and wholly more universal (*omnes omnia omnino*): language teaching represented in his system only the first step on the road to real wisdom. This educational philosophy and scheme, the so called 'pansophy', was proposed by him as the only remedy for ailing humanity, as the true exit from the 'labyrinths of the world', the right way to 'universal enlightenment', and consequently and gradually the means to establish the perfect 'Christian society' (a free, peaceful and prosperous community of all nations).

Many of his contemporaries (especially in England and the German-speaking Reformed states) admired and supported his ambitious plans which partly resulted from the millenarian mystical traditions of the European as well as the Czech Reformation. However, there were scholars (among them Descartes and the Cartesians) who criticized his fusion of sciences and theology as doubtful and misleading, while some diehard Protestant divines (both Lutheran and Calvinist) found his theosophy dangerously heretical and socially destabilizing.

Nevertheless, when he died in 1670 he was much esteemed, although he was better known abroad than in his homeland where the victorious Hapsburgs tried to wipe out the memory of the native Reformation. But even Comenius's arch-enemies, the Jesuits, respected his educational achievements by printing his textbook *Janua linguarum* in Prague.

The following era of enlightenment, however, pushed Comenius into oblivion. The age of reason condemned Comenius's pansophy as a misleading and misguided philosophical concept. At the end of the seventeenth century, the French rationalist Pierre Bayle created in his influential *Dictionnaire Critique* a distorted image of Comenius. His sarcastic and ironic picture of the Czech reformer presented an unflattering caricature: here was a man of doubtful mental abilities who might, perhaps, write a few good textbooks but was otherwise a dangerous religious sectarian and fake, fanatically spreading foolish revelations and permanently searching for money from his naïve patrons. The former Huguenot Bayle, like many converts, condemned in Comenius his own past and his former friends in Dutch exile (the *Dictionnaire* was published soon after the Revocation of the Edict of Nantes in 1697). Bayle had been a leading Huguenot theologian and in his youth he believed in similar revelations. Bayle's portrait of Comenius became generally accepted. His *Dictionnaire* was reprinted several times and translated into German.

At the end of the eighteenth century the German literary wit Adelung chose Comenius as a striking and infamous example for his popular book *Geschichte der menschlichen Narrheit* (*History of human foolishness*). Comenius, it seemed, was destined for ridicule if not oblivion: even his textbooks were published less frequently. The bicentenary of his birth (in 1792) was not remembered. His spiritual legacy survived only in small Bohemian groups exiled in Germany. These partly inspired the German pietistic movement (A.H. Francke in Halle) and the newly founded Moravian Church in Saxonian Herrnhut (*Unitat der Mahrischen Bruder*).

Comenius's slow restoration to European cultural history is

closely associated with the new philosophical and literary movement, Romanticism. It was the German philosopher J.G. Herder who described Comenius as one of the most noble and magnificent spirits of Europe, a man whose reform endeavours should be highly appreciated. Similar evaluations were formulated by the French historian Jules Michelet, the Swiss educationalist Pestalozzi, and other influential Europeans.

Comenius finally found his way home into Bohemia and Moravia. His literary and theological works, especially those written in his mother tongue, were published for the first time after the Act of Toleration in 1781; and despite its continuing problems with censorship, Comenius's work became one of the chief sources of inspiration for Czech national revival in the nineteenth century.

The first modern biography of Comenius, written and published in 1829 (both in Czech and German) by the foremost Czech historian and politician, F. Palacky (son of a country Protestant teacher), pictured Comenius as above all a great patriot. This nationalistic image was a natural response to the official Viennese centralism and Germanization (Palacky, of course, considered Bohemian history as an everlasting struggle between 'Slav democracy' and 'Teutonic autocracy'). And so Comenius became a symbol of the anti-Hapsburg Bohemian tradition and national striving for independence. From that point of view it is not surprising that the Viennese government tried to prohibit the celebration of the tercentenary of his birth in 1892. These celebrations nevertheless became a cultural and political demonstration of national identity, led by the Czech intelligentsia. Czech teachers in particular adored Comenius as their great example—Comenius's portraits, statues and busts decorated almost every school built in the last third of the nineteenth century and this tendency has continued in our own century.

This enthusiastic portrait of a great Czech teacher, heading the Slav democrats in their struggle against Austrian-German oppression, was naturally very limited. Comenius was in fact bilingual, studying and living for many years in a German-speaking environment. He was, of course, a passionate and devoted patriot in seventeenth-century terms, but his patriotism was deeply associated with the Protestant faith, and that is why he preferred exile to the enforced conversions which his countrymen had to endure.

By the beginning of the twentieth century Comenius's work was again becoming internationally acknowledged. His writings have been reproduced in critical editions, not only in Bohemia but throughout Europe, translated from Latin and Czech into several modern European languages. This new, scholarly, approach (by Kvacala, Novak and Hendrich, for instance) stressed the educational values of his work. His philosophical and religious writings were considered by the positivist generation of the first half of the twentieth century to be less important; they were seen as controversial and obscure.

Postwar political and ideological changes adjusted the portrait of Comenius again into a new hagiographical frame. Unlike the nationalist idealization of the nineteenth century, the Marxist view, represented by the historian and first Communist minister of education, Z. Nejedly, and his close associate, the educationalist, O. Chlup, portrayed Comenius as a highly 'progressive' personality, anticipating (in spite of 'the reactionary religious disguise') socialist and communist school reforms and ideals. Comenius, pictured as not only anti-feudal but also latently anti-bourgeois and anti-capitalist, was placed in school-galleries of progressive revolutionary figures alongside Makarenko and Lenin. His ideas on human freedom, peace in liberty and Christian reformation were not, of course, remembered in official speeches or propagandist brochures.

The official recognition of Comenius as 'a pioneer of socialism' at least enabled in the 1950s the editing of his educational research (to a certain, ideologically limited, degree). After the late 1950s and early 1960s, the Czech cultural and intellectual scene, including historiography and Comeniology, underwent deep changes as a result of de-Stalinization. More reform-minded and sophisticated opinions influenced non-orthodox Marxist interpretations of Comenius's work and personality. R. Kalivoda, J. Polisensky and J. Popelova contributed substantially to the more complex philosophical and historical portrayal of Comenius. But even non-Marxist studies of Comenius (mostly from Protestant scholars) began to appear:

works of high quality are represented by the publications of J. Patocka and A. Molnar.

The general decline in humanitarian sciences after the revival of the Stalinist system in the early 1970s had a restrictive impact on Comenius research, although this 'harmless' issue—or so it seemed to the Party ideologists—was not closely observed by the party censors. (This is why scientific development was not interrupted to the same extent as research in modern history.) The review *Studia Comeniana et historica*, published by the Museum of J.A. Comenius in Uhersky Brod since 1974, became a platform for relatively free scholarly discussion (shadowed by the politically motivated publication-ban on such outstanding scholars as Patocka or Kalivoda). This comparatively open and scholarly spirit prevailed also in the regular Comeniological colloquia, organized every year by the small Moravian museum in Uhersky Brod, which has become the major and internationally respected centre of Comenius research. The Prague Academy of Sciences itself, despite these political setbacks, is gradually realizing its remarkably and ambitious programme, begun in 1969, of a complete edition of Comenius's writings.

Recent research, both in Czechoslovakia and abroad, contributes to a more rounded picture of this universal reformer and thinker whose work has both Czech and European roots and dimensions. Such interdisciplinary co-operation and interpretation seems to be a necessity in contemporary research.

The image of Comenius has always played an important political, cultural, psychological and emotional role in Czechoslovakia. It is significant that all three Czech democratic presidents (Masaryk, Beneš and Havel) appreciated Comenius's work for its humanistic values as a part of the common Czech-European heritage. Comenius's image has always been influenced by the current social and intellectual approaches. In his case there will be always a danger of hagiographical idealization, modernization and one-sided 'black-and-white' interpretations. But the quatercentenary of his birth in 1992 proved to be at once the obligatory official tribute to a great European scholar, and a spur in recreating a more colourful, plastic and truthful portrait.

# Daniel Defoe: Ministry, Academy, and Milieu. A Problem for Whom?

*Philip Mulreany*

## I

In general, London (perhaps because of its size and the vast volume of available records) has been under-emphasized in histories of the pre-Industrial Revolution period. This balance is now being redressed,[1] but the student might still be forgiven for seeing the Industrial Revolution as primarily concerned with developments in remote rural or newer urban locations from which London is either wholly or partially detached. The rebuilding of London after the Great Fire and Plague, and its growth as a market, port, manufacturing and services centre are rarely or inadequately linked to such developments.

In London throughout this period there were several identifiable and well-documented Dissenting communities and there is a wealth of archival material about them. This is particularly true of the communities in the north-to-northeast quadrant of Islington, Stoke Newington and Hackney.

A particular theme which calls for examination is the association between certain aspects of Dissenting culture and institutions and the development and sustaining of an 'entrepreneurial ethos'. In this context special attention should be paid to the contribution of the Dissenting Academy. A key figure in any assessment of this must be Daniel Defoe (c. 1660–1731), by virtue of his long residence in and near Stoke Newington, and

1. For example, at the Centre for Metropolitan History, University of London Institute for Historical Research.

his attendance at Dr Charles Morton's Academy at Newington Green (c. 1674–1679), about which he wrote.

The citation of Defoe and the Dissenting Academy as a source by social and economic historians has been a strong one. To T.S. Ashton, whose background was Congregationalist,

> the academies established by nonconformist zeal for education... were nurseries of scientific thought...and from them proceeded a stream of future industrialists...[2]

To P. Mathias, who dedicates his text to Ashton's memory,

> The Nonconformists developed their own schools—the Dissenting Academies—which provided the best education for a commercial career available in eighteenth-century England, having a very practical emphasis (with foreign languages, mathematics, accounting)...[3]

And Mathias refers particularly to

> Daniel Defoe, himself a dissenter from exactly this enclave of society from which so many entrepreneurs sprang, author of the *Essays on Projects*, the *Complete Tradesman*, the *Plan of English Commerce*, and the keenest observer of economic growth of his time in the *Tour of the Whole Island*, [who] expressed part of this personal, individual motivation of work, accumulation and enterprise in one of the best economic myths of the age, *Robinson Crusoe*. This was the characteristic response of minority groups who became key agents of economic growth in eighteenth century England.[4]

As Pat Rogers has noted, in their presentation of Defoe's material, these and other social and economic historians treat Defoe's work as that of the 'Great Reporter', a literalist and a journalistic observer. Their view of Defoe derives primarily from his *Tour through the whole Island of Great Britain*. Thus, for G.M. Trevelyan:

> When a survey is demanded of Queen Anne's England and its everyday life, our thoughts turn to Daniel Defoe, riding solitary and observant through the countryside...Defoe the trader hailed

2. T.S. Ashton, *The Industrial Revolution 1760–1830* (Oxford, 1970), p. 16.
3. P. Mathias, *The First Industrial Nation. An Economic History of Britain 1700–1914* (Methuen, 1969), pp. 158-59.
4. Mathias, *First Industrial Nation*, p. 161.

> the era of business...he first perfected the art of the reporter; even his novels such as *Robinson Crusoe* and *Moll Flanders* are imaginary reports of daily life, whether on a desert island or in a thieves' den. So then the account that this man gives of the England of Anne's reign is for the historian a treasure indeed. For Defoe was one of the first who saw the old world through a pair of sharp modern eyes. His report can be controlled and enlarged by great masses of other evidence, but it occupies the central point of our thought and vision.[5]

And for Dorothy George:

> For the best authority for early eighteenth-century England is Defoe. His famous *Tour through the whole Island of Great Britain* shows us the country as it appeared to a skilled observer with a marvellous eye for significant detail, who was also a man of business and a consummate journalist.[6]

As Rogers notes, large parts of Paul Mantoux's *The Industrial Revolution in the Eighteenth Century* and Cole and Postgate's *The Common People* depend on Defoe. Christopher Hill, Sir John Clapham, the Hammonds, and E. Lipson have also cited Defoe's work extensively as a primary source. Yet, Defoe's legion of biographers and other Defoe scholars seem rarely, if ever, referred to.

5. G.M. Trevelyan, *Illustrated Social History: 3* (Harmondsworth: Penguin, 1966), p. 17 (opening ch. 1 on 'Defoe's England'). In fact, Defoe was not solitary, as Pat Rogers reminds us:

> I took with me an *ancient Gentleman* of my Acquaintance, who I found was thorowly acquainted with almost every Part of *England*, and who was to me as a walking Library, or a moveable Map of the Countries and Towns through which we pass'd;

Cited by Rogers in her introduction to D. Defoe, *A Tour through the whole Island of Great Britain* (Penguin, 1971), p. 34. There is also a strong case for interpreting *Robinson Crusoe* and *Moll Flanders* as autobiography (cf. G.A. Starr, *Defoe and Spiritual Autobiography* [Princeton University Press, 1965]) rather than as imaginary reports of daily life.

6. D. George, *England in Transition. Life and Work in the Eighteenth Century* (Harmondsworth: Penguin, 1969), p. 29 (opening ch. 11 on 'Defoe's England: London and the Country'). It must be said that, as a businessman, Defoe was at least twice bankrupted, 1692 and 1706, and was pursued to his death by the Assignee of a creditor; as a journalist, his work was never mere reportorial observation as inspection of the *Review* quickly shows.

Of course, when Defoe is cited the impression is given that he is not reliable in every detail. He sometimes confuses generations in families, gets names wrong, gets his population estimates wrong...But these very deficiencies serve only to strengthen one's view of the integrity of the historian who is citing him. They give an impression that only marginal problems are being encountered. Thus Defoe has remained a credible and frequent source for all students of the England which immediately preceded the Industrial Revolution.

## II

To Rogers, this view of Defoe is not merely partial and inadequate, it is also based on false premisses. More recently, P.N. Furbank and W.R. Owens have shown that it runs counter to a considerable amount of biographical research, and G.A. Starr has shown it to be inconsistent with autobiographical research.

Much of Defoe's apparent journalism, like his correspondence, was in fact satirical, combative and deeply imaginative. In his time he was charged as 'the great fabricator'. Rogers believed it to be wholly wrong to see the *Tour* as in some way separated from Defoe's major literary works: 'The Tour embodies all Defoe's accumulated skills as chronicler, polemicist and creative writer. It is, in short, a deeply imaginative book.'[7]

Conversely, it seems ironic that Defoe's apparently 'fictional' output should be regarded as separable from 'journalistic' works. Indeed, much of Defoe's verifiably fictional output is also satirical, allegorical and, quite often, autobiographical. Defoe scholars have for some years been in disarray over this, which renders even more surprising the confident approach of the economic and social historians.

The important work of P.N. Furbank and W.R. Owens, *The Canonisation of Daniel Defoe*,[8] reiterates the feeling, shared by a number of scholars, that the Defoe canon is in fact a strange and unsatisfactory construction. They believe that not all the

7. Rogers (ed.), *Tour*, p. 10.

8. P.N. Furbank and W.R. Owens, *The Canonisation of Daniel Defoe* (Yale University Press, 1988).

work attributed to Defoe could possibly be his, any more than could all the professional attributes of Defoe, the objective journalist. Furbank and Owens speculate that something fundamental may have gone wrong—an early error, perhaps, begetting years of further errors, or possibly the faulty use of the basic principles of attribution. Perhaps something similar occurred in the work of our social and economic historians. Furbank and Owens remind us that the largest part of Defoe's work was published anonymously or pseudonymously and that, although (in)famous in his time, it was not until sixty years after his death that any serious attempt was made to draw up a full list of his writings. In effect a lifetime had passed, and that first attempt by Chalmers was itself speculative. Further biographers so extended it that 'between 1790 and 1970 the Defoe Canon had swollen from 101 items to 570'.[9] They note how this growth so disturbed Donald Wing, the compiler of the *Short Title Catalogue* for 1641/1700, that he offered his successor this simple solution to handling anonymous early eighteenth-century works: 'I suggest to my followers the commonsense of putting them all under Daniel Defoe. If we keep on adding twenty or thirty a year to his *corpus*, wouldn't it be time-saving to admit now that he probably wrote them all?'[10]

Most subsequent attributions are based on less than satisfactory internal stylistic evidence and, since Chalmers, they have been the work of a few notable, yet idiosyncratic, individuals. Furbank and Owens argue strongly for a radical re-appraisal of current attribution. They believe that even if the present checklist is to be trusted, there remain major problems of internal consistency.

> we must believe that Defoe, who wrote *Robinson Crusoe* and other great novels and who, in his *Review*...produced prose of great verve, intellectual grasp and polemical edge, would also produce pamphlets of unfathomable dullness or asininity, incompetent and bungling historical narratives, and quite characterless hackwork compilations.[11]

9. Furbank and Owens, *Canonisation*, pp. 2-3.
10. Furbank and Owens, *Canonisation*, p. 3, from W.L. Lee, *Daniel Defoe: His Life, and Recently Discovered Writings* (3 vols.; 1869), I, p. xxiv.
11. Furbank and Owens, *Canonisation*, pp. 5-6.

They conclude: 'One would be hard put to discern any pattern...unless it be the pattern of systematic self-contradiction.'[12] But, in examining 'Defoe the man', they summarize the work of other scholars as suggesting contradictory views which far transcend the portrait of an 'objective journalist': he was, variously,

1) Protean
2) A brilliant and highly paid propagandist...
3) A low mercenary hack...
4) A workaholic...
5) A gratuitous and incorrigible hoaxer.[13]

All these views have an extreme quality, indeed the third was most persistently laid against Defoe in his lifetime; but none is consistent with the view of Defoe as the literalist, objective, journalist.

## III

So what, in fact, can we be sure that Defoe has to say about the academies and the ministry?

We must recall that the Act of Uniformity (1662) not only drove out a large number of ministers from livings in the Church of England, but it also closed the English universities to Nonconformists.[14] Ministers were not only forbidden to preach, they were also forbidden to teach. The Five Mile Act (1665) effectively tried to prevent ejected ministers from earning their livings by teaching or acting as tutors in the families of their former congregations. A number of ejected ministers had nevertheless opened schools although the Act forbade them to teach anywhere under a penalty of £40. It was at this time, and for this reason, that the first Nonconformist ministers founded academies, later to be known collectively as the 'Dissenting

12. Furbank and Owens, *Canonisation*, p. 8.
13. Furbank and Owens, *Canonisation*, pp. 8-9.
14. Statutes of the Realm Vi, pp. 364-70, *An Act for the Uniformity of Public Prayers and Administration of Sacraments and other Rites and Ceremonies; and for establishing the Form of Making, Ordaining and Consecrating Bishops, Priests and Deacons in the Church of England.*

Academies'. Notwithstanding the Five Mile Act, the Dissenting Academies were unusually numerous in North London, where the earliest were kept by ejected clergy with unusually distinguished academic careers. At first persecution made it necessary to move frequently; and when the minister moved, as far as possible he would take his academy with him.[15] Islington, and the neighbouring parish of Stoke Newington, were favoured locations for these institutions.

The largest academy of the Presbyterians was that founded by Charles Morton,[16] at Stoke Newington Green from about 1675 to 1706. Morton had been a Fellow of Wadham College, Oxford, but he was persecuted so continuously that he went to New England in 1685 to become Vice-President of Harvard. Defoe was at the academy in Morton's time, and spoke well of his school, in response to Swift's contemporary criticisms of himself and Tutchin as 'two stupid illiterate scribblers'.[17] Defoe had retorted to Swift that, if he were a blockhead, it was not the fault of his father who had 'spared nothing in his education that might qualify him to match the accurate Dr Browne, or the learned Observator'.[18] Defoe's father, a member of Dr Annesley's congregation, intended his son for the Dissenting ministry, yet 'It is not often that I trouble you with any of my divinity. It was my disaster first to be set apart for, and then to be set apart from, that sacred employ.'[19]

He seems to have been placed in the academy at the age of fourteen and probably remained there for the full course of five years (c. 1674–1679). He has himself explained why, when his training was complete, he did not proceed to office in the pulpit,

15. E. Routley, *English Religious Dissent* (Cambridge: Cambridge University Press, 1960), p. 137; H. McLachlan, *English Education Under the Test Acts* (1933), pp. 2-10; I. Parker, *Dissenting Academies* (Cambridge: Cambridge University Press, 1914), pp. 57, 158.

16. *Dictionary of National Biography*; E. Calamy, *Continuation of Ejected Ministers* (1727), I, pp. 177-97 (Dr Williams's Library).

17. *Review*, vol. VII, No. 114, Saturday 16 December 1710; reproduced in W.L. Payne (ed.), *The Best of Defoe's Review. An Anthology* (Columbia University Press, 1951).

18. See n. 17.

19. Defoe, *More Short Ways with the Dissenters* (1705), pamphlet in Dr Williams's Library.

but changed his views and resolved to engage in business as a hose merchant. The sum of the explanation is that ministry seemed to him to be 'neither honourable, agreeable, nor profitable'.[20] It was degraded, he thought, by the entrance of men who had neither the physical nor the intellectual qualifications for it, who had received out of a denominational fund only such an education as made them pedants rather than Christian gentlemen of high learning, and who had consequently to submit to shameful and degrading practices in their efforts to obtain congregations and subsistence. Additionally, the behaviour of congregations to their ministers, who were dependent on their good will, was often objectionable and unchristian. Further, the 'prizes' of ministry in London were often given to strangers albeit 'eminent ministers called from all parts of England; some even from Scotland, finding acceptance in the metropolis before having received any formal ordination'.[21] Though his 'fund-bred' contemporaries, as he called them, excited Defoe's contempt, Defoe defends Dr Morton's excellence as a teacher, and instances the names of several preachers who did credit to his labours (including one Timothy Crusoe, and Samuel Wesley).[22]

However, there was a strong emphasis on written dissertations and on holding all disputations in English. This resulted, Defoe says, in pupils who, 'not destitute in languages', were yet 'made masters of the English tongue, and more of them excelled in that particular than at any school at that time'.[23] Whether in fact Defoe obtained at Newington Green the rudiments of all the learning he afterwards claimed is not certain, but his later claims should not be misinterpreted.[24]

Specifically when the taunt was again levelled at him, by the

20. Defoe, *Present State of the Parties in Great Britain* (1712), pp. 295-96, 315-17.

21. Defoe, *Present State*, pp. 295-96.

22. Defoe, *Present State*, pp. 295-96.

23. Defoe, *Present State*, pp. 295-96.

24. See *Review*, vol. II, No. 35, Thursday 31 May, 1705 ('Mr Review defends Mr Defoe') and vol. VII, No. 114, Saturday 16 December, 1710 (*Idiot Review* and *Scurrilous Examiner*), reproduced in Payne (ed.), *Best of Defoe's Review*.

university-educated Swift, of being an 'illiterate fellow'[25] and no scholar, in 1705, he protested that 'he had been in his time pretty well master of five languages, and had not lost them yet, though he wrote no bill at his door, nor set Latin quotations at the front of the "Review".'[26] It is not possible to establish whether in fact this knowledge was gained at the academy, and Defoe is consistently critical of the academies and their products. Indeed, if there are inconsistencies in Defoe's canon, it is not in evidence here.

> 'Tis evident the great imperfection of our academies is want of conversation: this, the public Universities enjoy; ours cannot. If a man pores upon his book he comes out a pedant, a mere scholar, rough and unfit for anything outside the walls of his college.
>
> ...Many of the tutors in our academies...tie down their pupils so exactly and limit them so strictly...that, at the end of the severest term of study, they come out unacquainted [with English].
>
> ...Many excellent ministers drive away their congregations with their sermons, while a jingling noisy boy, that has a good stock in his face and a dyssentry of the tongue, though he has little or nothing in his head, shall run away with the whole town.[27]

All the early academies were 'open', admitting Anglicans as well as training a proportion of students for the Dissenting ministry.

The reign of Queen Anne, with her natural preference for those who were zealous for the Church of England, saw a number of savage attacks launched against these centres. Already, in a sermon of 1685, Prebendary South had besought his hearers to 'employ the utmost of your power and interest...to suppress, to utterly suppress and extinguish, those private blind conventicling schools or academies,...set up and taught secretly by fanatics here and there the kingdom over'.[28]

Almost immediately after William III's death, the Church Party moved to suppress the Dissenting Academies. In November 1702, a Bill for preventing Occasional Conformity was introduced

25. Payne (ed.), *Best of Defoe's Review*, p. 91.
26. Payne (ed.), *Best of Defoe's Review*, p. 93.
27. Defoe, *Present State*, pp. 295-96.
28. A. Dale, *A History of English Congregationalism* (London, 1907), pp. 502-503.

to the House of Commons. This move was fomented in Queen Anne's first speech: 'as her Education and Choice had effectually ty'd her to the Church of England, so those who were Most Zealous for that Church, would be the persons she would most regard...'[29]

The fiercest denunciations of the academies came from Dr Henry Sacheverell, in sermons preached at Oxford in 1702. Sacheverell railed against the academies as 'dangerous to Church and State', and 'fountains of lewdness...[which] spawned all descriptions of heterodox, lewd and atheistical books'.[30] Although a product of Morton's Academy, Samuel Wesley attacked the academies for perpetuating a race of mortal enemies to Church and State, guilty of schism and sedition, drawing men away from the Church, and endangering the prosperity of the two universities. Dissenters were 'villains', 'hypocrities' and 'murderers'; he estimated that there were 'some thousands' among the pupils, 'sons of the nobility and gentry who, but for these sucking academies, would have gone to Oxford or Cambridge'.[31]

Defoe's response was *The Shortest Way with the Dissenters*, a pamphlet of such irony that, for a time, it deceived both those for whom it was written, and the Dissenters. Many members of the Church Party hailed it as their own production.[32] When the

29. *House of Commons Journals* xvii 636.

30. Dale, *English Congregationalism*, p. 503.

31. Dale, *English Congregationalism*, p. 502; John Wesley's *Letter from a Country Divine, concerning the education of Dissenters in their Private Academies, etc* was as unscrupulous and abusive as Sacheverell's reported sermons. Replies to Wesley and Sacheverell were made by Mr Samuel Palmer of Southwark and Mr James Owen as well as Defoe. Further comments were added by Defoe in *More Short Ways with the Dissenters* (1705), that are specific to Wesley.

32. Oldmixon gives the following story of a bookseller 'having an order from a Fellow of a College in Cambridge for a Parcel of Books, just at the time of publishing this *Shortest Way*, put up one of them in the Bundle not doubting it would be welcome to his customer; who accordingly thanked him for packing so excellent a Treatise up with the rest, it being next to the *Sacred Bible*, and *Holy Comments*, the best book he ever saw; but understanding afterwards it was written by a Rank Independent, he rail'd at it as much as he had extoll'd it, and forbad his Bookseller to send him any more Pamphlets without particular Order', *History of England*, etc. (1735), p. 301.

true authorship of the pamphlet was discovered, the Government (encouraged by an enraged clergy) brought Defoe to trial at the Old Bailey on 24 February 1703. He was fined 200 marks, sentenced to stand three times in the pillory, and to be imprisoned in Newgate 'during the Queen's pleasure'. Defoe was extracted from this incarceration by Robert Harley. In return and in effect, he became a paid informer and a spy.[33]

His correspondence with Harley and others is particularly revealing about his views of Dissenting Academies and the Dissenting ministry. They seem remarkably entrenched. He clearly felt himself ill-used by his fellow Dissenters: 'Even the Dissenters...lift up the first dagger at me: I confess it makes me Reflect on the wholl body of the Dissenters with Something of Contempt More Than Usuall, and gives me the More Regret that I Suffer for Such a People.'[34] Defoe's views seem to change little in this correspondence, with copious advice to Harley on 'Methods of Management of the Dissenters'.[35]

> I am Persuaded Freedom and favour to the Dissenters is the Directest method to Lessen their Numbers and bring them at last into the Church...
>
> The Dissenters are Divided and Impolitick...They Are Not form'd into a body as they are Onely Numbers Irregularly Mixt They are Uncapable of Acting in Any Capacity.
>
> The most that Ever they do is to Address by Their Ministers.[36]

Later, in a letter to Harley on Bolingbroke's 1714 Schism Bill, designed to embarrass Harley and bring about the total abolition of the Dissenting Academies,[37] Defoe maintains his view:

Henry Sacheverell (1674–1724) was Fellow of Magdalen, Oxford, a High Church Enthusiast and an enemy of occasional conformity. Defoe denounced him for several years in many satirical pamphlets.

33. See G.H. Healey (ed.), *The Letters of Daniel Defoe* (Oxford, 1955), *passim*.

34. Letter to William Patterson, April 1703, in Healey, *Letters*, p. 4.

35. Letter to Robert Harley, August–September 1704, in Healey, *Letters*, p. 51.

36. Healey, *Letters*, p. 54.

37. *House of Commons Journals* xvii 636.

First the Bill depending about The dissenters Schools, which I fear will pass; it is True my Lord the Conduct of the Dissenters has call'd for more Than this...
As to Their Academies, if there had never been any, I kno' not but Theyr intrest had been as Good, and Fewer beggars an Drones had been bred up for Ministers Among Them...

The Dissenters have Now become to Reflect upon their Indolence and Supine Negligence, who at the Revolution when They Obtain'd the Tolleration, Took no Thought for the Education of their Posterity, of a Succession of Ministers to Preach to Them;...[38]

As it happened, the Schism Bill failed to achieve the Royal Assent because of Queen Anne's death.

With the establishment of some measure of accommodation after the death of Anne, and the birth of ministerial Training Boards, the emphasis of teaching became more overtly vocational.[39] Samuel Pike, for example, from about 1750 received only theological students at his house in Hoxton Square.[40] Curricula reflected this, with higher weightings given to divinity, rhetoric, and Jewish antiquities. The academies suddenly became pioneers in the development of the later theological colleges. Indeed in North London they left few permanent institutions other than theological colleges.

The abuses of which Defoe had complained, continued long after his death. A number of English Dissenting ministers received their doctorates from Scottish universities. However, Lincoln argues that, towards the end of the eighteenth century, the practice of dispensing such degrees had become disreputable;[41] when Robert Robinson, a celebrated Baptist minister

38. Healey, *Letters*, pp. 440-41.

39. Eventually one group of academies merged in 1852 to form New College, Swiss Cottage. These included Highbury College, which in turn represented the mergers of the 'Societas Evangelica' from Hoxton, Stepney and Bethnal Green. Also involved were the 'King's Head Academy' which by then had become Homerton College, and Coward College Bloomsbury (successor to Phillip Doddridge's Academy at Northampton).

40. McLachlan, *English Education*, p. 2.

41. A. Lincoln, *The Dissenting Interest 1763–1800* (Cambridge: Cambridge University Press, 1938), pp. 73-74.

who lectured briefly in London around 1780[42] was offered a Doctorate of Divinity by the University of Edinburgh, he considered that 'So many egregious dunces have been made DDs, both in English as well as in Scotch and American Universities, that he declined the compliment'.[43]

## IV

Does Defoe's consistency in this show in his fictional literature also?

It is possible to agree with Starr's analysis that *Robinson Crusoe* (and to a lesser extent *Moll Flanders* and *Roxanna*) are strongly influenced by a long tradition of spiritual autobiography. Defoe's novels were, of course, written when he was over sixty years old, and are reflective.[44] Particularly important is the view that Crusoe's solitary confinement to the Island is God's punishment for Crusoe's great 'sin' of defying the wishes of his father (God's natural representative in the family) and seeking to evade the calling given him by providence. All that subsequently befalls him was caused by his

> apparent obstinate adhering to my foolish inclination of wandering abroad and pursuing that inclination, in contradiction to the clearest views of doing myself good in a fair and plain pursuit of those projects and measures of life which nature and providence concurred to present me with, and to my duty.[45]

As Angus Ross has pointed out,[46] the conventional analysis of economists has not been particularly helpful in interpreting this literature. The tendency to use these works as a quarry for earlier ideas on economic doctrine has been replicated by social and religious quarrying.

Starr has convincingly shown that

42. *Dictionary of National Biography*.

43. G. Dyer, *Memoirs of the Life and Writings of Robert Robinson* (London, 1796), p. 199.

44. Starr, *Defoe and Spiritual Autobiography*, pp. 74-125.

45. Cited by A. Ross (ed.), *The Life and Strange Surprising Adventuries of Robinson Crusoe of York, Mariner...* (Harmondsworth: Pelican, 1971), p. 14.

46. Ross (ed.), *Robinson Crusoe*, pp. 14-17.

> many of Defoe's religious attitudes are less distinctively or exclusively Puritan than they are commonly taken to be...By a comparison of statements made in different contexts, in different decades, by authors of different denominations, it becomes clear that the leading religious ideas in Defoe's fiction were in fact commonplaces of the English protestant tradition, not merely crotchets of the much-discussed Dissenting milieu.[47]

Seen thus, Defoe's spiritual-autobiographical novels remain wholly consistent with Defoe's broadened Protestantism.

V

How then, might Defoe's Protestantism have broadened? Despite his occasional satires on the 'sin' of Occasional Conformity, it is clear that Defoe himself conformed, at least occasionally, and undertook minor vestry offices willingly. It is similarly harder to obtain any evidence after his pillorying of regular attendance at any particular Dissenting meeting.

In 1717 he was elected one of the surveyors of the highways by the Vestry of the parish of St Mary, Stoke Newington. He apparently accepted the office for there is no evidence of the payment of a customary fine to avoid the duties. The minute book read

> At a Vestry holden for the parish of Stoke Newington in the county of Middlesex this 26th Day of Decemb 1717. The former order of vestry made is confirmed—the choice of Surveyors of the Highways for the year ensuing by Majority of Votes fell on and they were Returned to the Justices
>
> Daniel De Foe
> John Hewett
> John Whitty[48]

In contrast, in 1712, the following entry appeared in the minute book:

> Att a vestery holden for the parish of Stoke Newington in the County of Middlesex this 10th day of April 1721 Being Easter

47. Starr, *Defoe and Spiritual Autobiography*, Preface, p. xi.

48. Cited by A.J. Shirren, *Daniel Defoe in Stoke Newington* (Stoke Newington Borough Council, 1965).

> Monday for ye choosing Churchwardens and Overseers of ye Poor for ye year ensuing—the choyce fell upon
>
> Captain J$^{no}$ Whitty
> Mr Dan Deffoe
>
> A motion being made to make an Estimate of ye Debts of the Parish It was accordingly dun and it was found to amount to Sixty Pounds or thear about. Referd to conceder how to rate ye Money next Vestery, Mr Daniel deffoe haveing desired to be admitted to a fine to excuse him all offices upon pan$^{t}$ of Tenn Pounds. It is agreed to accept of it.[49]

A.J. Shirren notes that it has been suggested that in order to raise money the vestry was wont to elect well-to-do Nonconformists knowing they would rather pay a fine than serve their term of office. But Shirren doubts whether this was so in Defoe's case. The wording of the minute rather suggests that Defoe himself had put forward the idea of paying a fine to be excused of '*all* offices'; not only the one to which he had been elected.

Further, when Sir John Hartopp, the leading local Nonconformist, was elected churchwarden, he was excused service without payment of a fine. Shirren concludes that the local vestry may very well have intended these elections as compliments to well-known local residents.

## VI

There thus appears to be a clear case for review with respect to several interpretations of Defoe's work.

Any misrepresentation of Defoe based on a highly selective use of his works, whether as sources for description, social, economic or religious ideas is certainly to be regretted. Most importantly, the presentation of Defoe as a paradigm of the Dissenting culture immediately before the Industrial Revolution, cannot seriously be sustained, on its current basis. Impossible to sustain, given Defoe's strictures, is the old view that the Dissenting Academies represented some sort of business school, unique to that culture. Such representations have seriously

49. Shirren, *Defoe in Stoke Newington*.

hindered our understanding of the relationships between early Puritanism, later Nonconformity, and contemporary Anglicanism, on the one hand, and of the processes of urbanization and industrialization on the other. These remain only partially and imperfectly understood.

In seeking better understanding, the deficiencies of the canon must be borne in mind. Even so, on the specific issues of Dissenting Academies and ministerial training, it would seem that Defoe is consistent in his writings. He was intended for the ministry, was sent to an academy as a ministerial scholar and rejected it as a calling. That he rejected it on principle, and minimized the calling, academies, ministers, and (broadly) Dissenters for much of his life is indisputable. Even towards his life's end he describes this calling sarcastically as 'the upper station of low life',[50] and appears to have, at least occasionally, conformed.

Yet to reject Defoe as a paradigm of early eighteenth-century culture may be equally wrong. What is necessary at this stage is to form a clearer view of the whole man and his work, and to adopt a broader, more comprehensive view of its robustness as a source.

50. Ross (ed.), *Robinson Crusoe*, p. 14.

## The Awkwardness of Finding a Saint in Eighteenth-Century Geneva: Rousseau's Troublesome Holiness*

*Linda M. Kirk*

Eighteenth-century Calvinism was—for the most part—clear that the age of saints, like the age of miracles, was over. Less rational peoples in remote eras might need to be swept or bludgeoned into faith by evidence which contradicted commonsense; in enlightened Geneva it was thought unlikely that God would want to play fast and loose with science and by the same token it was presumed that he would not need the huge but mostly misshapen personalities of the particularly holy. Ordered energy flowing through acceptable channels was what Geneva wanted.

Jean-Jacques Rousseau posed no threat to his compatriots' expectations before 1754. His birth and childhood, his running away and conversion to Roman Catholicism, may not have been unremarkable,[1] but pointed to nothing which could become the

* The author acknowledges with thanks the assistance of the British Academy and the Research Fund of the University of Sheffield.

1. Jean-Jacques Rousseau (1712–1778), b. Geneva, left aged 16, converting to Roman Catholicism. After a wandering life, acquiring an education, he reached Paris, became a friend of Diderot and hoped to make his name through a new system of musical notation. After a brief spell as a favoured newcomer to the ranks of the *philosophes*, he denounced them and their 'programme', arguing in the *Discourse on the Arts and Sciences* that civilization corrupts humanity. In 1754 he revisited Geneva, re-entering its church. His *Discourse on the Origin of Inequality*, 1755, followed; as did a series of ruptures with former friends. *La Nouvelle Héloïse* (1761) was rapturously received; the governments of Europe banned and burned *l'Emile* and *Du*

focus for the longings of those who stayed at home. That his religious musings took him towards a loose but earnest deism like that of his own Savoyard vicar again made him nothing out of the ordinary—so far as the evidence allows us to judge—in eighteenth-century Europe. Protestants and Catholics alike were apt to take that route. A hint of what was to come can be seen in the awe-struck gullibility with which Rousseau was allowed readmission to the faith and city of his birth in 1754: somehow he was judged too famous or too sensitive to be subjected to the usual, rather firm, questioning which apostates underwent.[2]

Thereafter it was his sensibility, his deliberate cultivation and recording of fine feelings, which inflamed his contemporaries. His letters show that this did not come upon him suddenly, but the reading public was bowled over by the impact of *La Nouvelle Héloïse*.[3] The novel seemed to demonstrate that 'conventional' morality was not only an inadequate basis for living intensely, but could somehow be transcended by those convinced of their own core of righteousness. Within a year *l'Emile* and *Du Contrat Social* had extended the implications of this doctrine from flirtation and marriage to catechisms and politics.

Had Rousseau simply declared himself an outsider, emancipated from the constraints of Christian belief, he would have posed a much smaller threat. What he in fact did was to claim to be a more responsible citizen than the men who ruled Geneva, a more authoritative voice on the nature of the family than men

*Contrat Social* (1762) as irreligious and seditious. Rousseau fled into exile, first to territories belonging to Berne, then to Neuchâtel, then to England and at last back to France. Studies of Rousseau abound. Michel Launay, *Jean-Jacques Rousseau: Ecrivain Politique (1712–62)* (Grenoble: L'Association pour un Co-opérative d'Edition et de Recherche, 1971) offers an account which concentrates on his intellectual formation, taking due note of Rousseau's Genevan background and childhood.

2. E. Ritter, 'La Rentrée de Rousseau dans l'église de Genève', *Le Chrétien Evangelique* 11 (1884), pp. 153-98.

3. Robert Darnton, 'Readers respond to Rousseau: the fabrication of romantic sensitivity', in *The Great Cat Massacre* (Bungay, Suffolk: Penguin Books, 1984), pp. 225-27, 235-42; and see more than twenty letters in R.A. Leigh (ed.), Rousseau's *Correspondance Complète*, VIII (Geneva: Institut et Musée Voltaire; and Madison: Wisconsin University Press, 1969).

who married their women and brought up their children, yet more Christian than the clergy. That his insights had been attained through tears and suffering gave credibility to his claims. Like Jesus, he was apt to tell people they could not serve two masters. He was a professional polarizer, and that is where the danger lay.

His own *Confessions* are the best-known biography of Rousseau, and all later commentators have had to draw on it. The book makes great play with the unique inwardness of what it records; Rousseau leads the reader along what are normally hidden pathways of the mind; he claims to experience everything more vividly than ordinary people. His judgments on the conduct of others are often brisk and unforgiving; his own behaviour is always explained and justified from the privileged vantage point of the only spectator with access to the truth about his motives. When verifiable details—dates, times and places—have been checked against other records, a significant number of them have been proved wrong.[4] Scholars do not agree about the extent to which this calls in question the validity of those parts of the work which cannot be checked.

Those with whom Rousseau had quarrelled felt threatened by the knowledge that, from 1765 onwards, he was composing this account of himself. Rousseau's detailed, frantic recollections of friendships gone sour were bound to make compelling reading. Indeed, Rousseau went public more uninhibitedly than they feared: back in Paris in 1771 after his exile he gave readings from the work to adoring salon audiences. On the other hand, he kept his pledge of silence about the events of the quarrel with Hume, and the *Confessions* (as it has come to us) stops abruptly in 1765. A third volume was threatened, but never appeared.

It is the purpose of this essay not to review the *Confessions* or to evaluate its usefulness for understanding Rousseau's life and times, but to establish two things: first, that long before this account was published he had constructed and successfully

4. Maurice Cranston, *Jean-Jacques: the early Life and Work of Jean-Jacques Rousseau* (London: Allen Lane, 1983), p. 9 and for instance pp. 93-94, 150-52, 307; *Correspondance*, I (Geneva: Institut et Musée Voltaire, 1965), p. 10, note b, p. 15, note d.

publicized his persona, and secondly, that throughout the 1760s Rousseau sought disciples rather than mere friends or admirers, thus fascinating and dividing Geneva.

When he made his much-discussed return to the city in 1754 he was received as a celebrity, a man of consequence about whom people knew only a few key facts, and little to his discredit. Somehow he had become known not just through works in print, but through 'private' letters which received wider currency than such letters normally do, and through gossip and legend. Rather than itemize fragments of information, their route to Geneva and their apparent impact, what follows will identify facets of the Rousseau-product, establish what was unnerving about it for his more conventional compatriots and show that the harm it was later to cause sprang directly from his claims to holiness.

Rousseau claimed to be poor, and on the side of the poor, if not actually poor in spirit. He was, he said, rejected by the great and worldly: persecuted for righteousness' sake. He was meek; he mourned. He was pure in heart and hungered and thirsted after righteousness. The rhythms of the beatitudes press his claim; those whom Jesus had called *'bênis'* must be at least apprenticed to sanctity. Rousseau could not convincingly present himself as a peace-maker nor as especially merciful, but even his incomplete match with the Christian ideal was close enough to be uncomfortable for his critics. He projected a disenchantment with 'civilization', with the urban life of Paris, the salons, the glittering literati and the chattering classes which would have seemed cynical if it had sprung from satiety. What he claimed, however, was that he had seen through the falseness of the Enlightenment's confidence: its hopes to reform the world rested on a misapprehension. Knowledge could not heal. Or rather, scientific knowledge merely made clearer the sordid tangle of self-interests which sustained the present order. Nothing less than the restructuring of the maimed human heart would do. From this would follow a fresh start to history.

The claim was Christ-like. Rousseau consciously drew on the gospels, and used their language. It was a way of wrong-footing those who rejected him and was clear evidence that he hungered for righteousness. How well-founded were his claims to be poor, pure and persecuted?

Rousseau's poverty was a fact. Before his death he was to have rejected pensions from the kings of France, England and Prussia: in the 1750s only Louis XV had made the unwanted offer.[5] Rousseau's family money was no great fortune, and little of it reached him; in 1737 he collected some 6,500 florins remaining from his mother's estate, and in 1747 rather less after his father's death.[6] For most of his contemporaries, these sums would have represented fabulous wealth, but Rousseau had—at that time—a taste for elegant living. The income he made from his various salaried posts was limited, and short-lived; his writings were to bring in more money, though without security. After his 'reform' he decided his only way of earning a living without dependence was music-copying. This took long hours, but was not in any other way equivalent to the toil endured by the peasants of eighteenth-century Europe even though he spoke as if from their perspective in the passionate rhetoric of the *Discours sur les Richesses*.[7] When Rousseau was in exile in the 1760s he was—as always—suspicious of benefactors, and careful to pay for goods ordered which kindly souls tried to give as presents, but amongst the commodities he required were coffee, and fine cloth for Thérèse. His was genteel rather than absolute poverty.[8]

Geneva's attitude towards poverty was ambivalent. The city had set its face against display and extravagance at the time of the Reformation, and had undergone real privations as recently as the 1690s. It possessed no vast estates; many of its great families had sprung only recently from penniless refugees. It ran a system of poor relief which gave intermittent support to more than a tenth of the population. But attitudes had moved a long

5. R.A. Leigh, 'Rousseau's English Pension', in J.H. Fox, M.H. Waddicor, D.A. Watts (eds.), *Studies in Eighteenth-Century French Literature presented to Robert Niklaus* (Exeter: University of Exeter, 1975).

6. Cranston, *Jean-Jacques*, pp. 125, 210.

7. 'Discours sur les Richesses', in *Fragments inédits suivis des residences de Jean-Jacques, par Alfred de Bougy, s. Bibliothécaire à la Sorbonne* (Paris: J. Dagneau, 1853), or, more accessibly, Rousseau, *Lettre à d'Alembert* (ed. Michel Launay; Paris: Garnier-Flammarion, 1967), pp. 184, 218, 244-45.

8. E.g. *Correspondance* (Banbury: Voltaire Foundation, 1973), XVIII, 3072; XIX, 3100, 3107.

way from respect for the holy poor: hard work was expected and required; quite a long way down the social scale, artisans invested money in property or funds.[9] In his communications with this group Rousseau made it plain he supported diligence rather than parasitism. Others in Geneva had prospered so far that they had no need to work. They could live as rentiers off the endeavours of others. The top 300–400 families enjoyed over a thousand florins a day,[10] while a workman and his family struggled to survive on two.[11] For them Rousseau's bias toward the poor sounded revolutionary. His respect for the individual's right to private property extended no further than the right to own enough, he was to explain in a note to *Contrat Social*.[12]

Purity likewise was subject to a special Rousseauesque interpretation. Julie, the heroine of *Nouvelle Héloïse,* threw away her virginity on her tutor (a figure strangely resembling Rousseau) but was for ever 'innocent' because her heart was good, and she meant no evil.

Eighteenth-century men, and eighteenth-century gentlemen in particular, were content with the sexual double standard. Even Geneva had not managed to sustain its even-handed ferocity against male and female misconduct for more than the first twenty years of the Reformation.[13] So Rousseau's long premarital association with Thérèse Lavasseur was odd only in that he chose finally to make an honest woman of her in 1768. But when he returned to Geneva in 1754 he managed not only to claim that their relationship was private and innocent, but to force those who thought otherwise on to the defensive: how dare they smear him and his nurse-companion with innuendo?

9. Patrick O'Mara, 'Geneva in the Eighteenth Century. A Socio-economic Study of the Bourgeois City-state during its Golden Age' (PhD thesis, University of California, 1954), pp. 100-102.

10. O'Mara, 'Golden Age', pp. 108-109.

11. Anne-Marie Piuz, 'Jean Vian (vers 1690–1772), ouvrier italien refugié à Genéve. Contribution à la typologie de la pauvreté ancienne', in *Studi in Memoria di Federigo Melis* (Naples: Gianni, 1978), IV, pp. 395-407.

12. Jean-Jacques Rousseau, *Du Contrat Social* (ed. R. Grimsley; Oxford: Clarendon Press, 1972), p. 172.

13. E. William Monter, 'Women in Calvinist Geneva (1550–1800)', *Signs: Journal of Women in Culture and Society* 6.2 (The University of Chicago, 1980), pp. 190-93.

It was the story of their five abandoned children which cost him the approval of more Genevans than he liked to recognize. Voltaire broke the news in *Sentiment des Citoyens*, a tasteless squib which, among other charges, alleged that Rousseau's painful urinary condition was the legacy of venereal disease.[14] This pamphlet, or at least the parts of it that were true, turned some responsible Genevans like the doctor Tronchin from sympathizers to enemies of Rousseau; the ill-will and the untruths, however, helped to confirm Rousseau's 'disciples' in their view that he was persecuted—which he was—and therefore holy—which did not follow.

What other persecution had Rousseau undergone? His version of his year with the French Ambassador in Venice was that he had been exploited, underappreciated and mistrusted. His friendship with Diderot broke up in acrimony; again Rousseau saw himself as the innocent victim. His stay at l'Hermitage had come to a disastrous end: he had fallen out with the Comtesse d'Houdetot, Madame d'Epinay, the Marquis de St-Lambert and Melchior Grimm. The details of this imbroglio were not widely known (indeed to this day agreed details are hard to establish), but somehow Rousseau had managed to present to the world a picture of himself as a man who had innocently provoked the unreasonable and adulterous group which had purported to be offering him friendship. Later quarrels, like that of 1766 with David Hume, proved more difficult for his Genevan followers to explain satisfactorily: du Peyrou wrote saying that he was of course convinced that all the fault must have been on Hume's side, but would Rousseau please account for a number of awkward points in the story? He would like to demonstrate rather than merely assert his friend's innocence.[15] This request detonated one of Rousseau's more powerful expositions of the view that anyone not with him was a perfidious enemy.[16] His meekness was of an uncommon kind, and did not extend to hearing unwelcome things said about his conduct or opinions.

14. *Sentiment des Citoyens* (Geneva: Cramer, 1765).

15. *Correspondance*, XXX (Oxford: Voltaire Foundation, Taylor Institute, 1977), 5431.

16. *Correspondance*, XXXI (Oxford: Voltaire Foundation, Taylor Institute, 1978), 5462.

What kept his followers loyal, awed and uncomfortable was Rousseau's passionate and eloquent mourning for the damage social arrangements had done to the innocence of man. He hungered and thirsted for righteousness; he was unembarrassed by the transcendent; he shamed reasonable moderate men into seeing themselves as timeservers; he presented property as theft and civility as deceit. Not all of this was apparent by 1754. For a while after his return visit to Geneva, in spite of his 'reform', Rousseau's fellow citizens were more likely to see him as the local boy with important connections, who might secure the best possible printing of the *Encyclopédie*, or a stylist who might help out with the new translation of the Bible.[17] There was talk of his settling in his home city, which was never to come about. Nonetheless he rushed to defend its unsophisticated civilization when d'Alembert's 1757 article suggested that Geneva needed a theatre, and a little more fun. In the *Lettre à d'Alembert sur les Spectacles* Rousseau presented an idealized picture of a city where middling people led decent lives, where men were men and women knew their place, where moderate humane clergy might indeed be drifting towards Socinianism but should not have that label pinned on them without their own direct testimony.[18]

So if in the late 1750s Rousseau and Geneva could ascribe sanctity to one another in warm mutual admiration, what made the 1760s so different? What led him to renounce his citizenship, and drove his Genevan supporters to denounce their rulers, challenging the political control of the oligarchy which ruled their city? There is no space here for the details of these events, but they amounted to a significant storm in a well-publicized

17. See Bibliothèque Publique et Universitaire de Genève: Registres de la Vénérable Compagnie, 1754; *Correspondance*, III (Geneva: Institut et Musée Voltaire, 1966), 401.

18. John Hope Mason, 'The *lettre à d'Alembert* and its place in Rousseau's thought', in M. Hobson, J.T. Leigh and R. Wokler (eds.), *Rousseau and the Eighteenth Century: Essays in Memory of R.A. Leigh* (Oxford: Voltaire Foundation, 1972). Rousseau thought that some societies, like that of Paris, were so far gone in corruption that plays and players might be defensible and might even represent a social safety value; Geneva on the other hand possessed a virtue worth preserving. Thus Rousseau sidestepped the awkward fact that he had himself written for the theatre.

teacup:[19] the campaign to vindicate Rousseau was to lead through a series of manoeuvres which, narrowly avoiding civil war, wrung some access for ordinary citizens to the governing circles in 1768.[20]

Predictably, the crisis turned on differing understandings of the pure heart, and what its rights were. On 9 June 1762 the Parlement of Paris banned and burned *l'Emile* and *Du Contrat Social*; on 19 June Geneva's Small Council followed suit. The books were judged seditious and irreligious. In summary, Rousseau's position was that since he was righteous, his writings could only be condemned by people who were wicked or who wilfully misread them. But even those members of the bourgeoisie who supported his political views were, for the most part, alarmed by what he taught on religion.[21] His readmission in 1754 began to look like a mistake; when the *curé* at Môtiers Travers allowed the new refugee to take Communion, he received stern letters from the Venerable Company of Pastors at Geneva.[22] The formal remonstrances, demonstrations and negotiations followed.

Rousseau was disappointed that most of his support came not from people who uncritically echoed his teaching, or deferred to his claims to see further and deeper than they could. Rather, old campaigners, alarmed about proper procedures and the doubtful legality of the measures taken against Rousseau, started to raise constitutional issues. Quite quickly the mode of discourse shifted from his to theirs: who governed Geneva? It was not even the case that the city's rulers could be charged with

19. Peter Gay, *Voltaire's Politics: The Poet as Realist* (Princeton: Princeton University Press, 1959), pp. 185-239 offers an accessible account in English of these events.

20. For this phase, see Jane Ceitac, 'Négociations sur le Projet Sécret de Tronchin avant le Projet de Conciliation de 1768', *Revue Suisse d'Histoire* 6 (1956), pp. 455-91, or, better, André Gür, 'La Négotation de l'Edit du 11 mars 1768, d'après le Journal de Jean-André De Luc et la Correspondance de Gédéon Turrettini', *Revue Suisse d'Histoire* 17 (1967), pp. 165-217.

21. See, for instance, A.J. Roustan, *Offrande aux Autels et à la Patrie* (Amsterdam: Marc Michel Rey, 1764), 'Defense du Christianisme en réfutation du Chapitre VIII du Contrat Social', pp. 1-95.

22. *Correspondance*, XIII (Geneva: Institut et Musée Voltaire, 1971), 2163, 2191, 2230.

illegally denying Rousseau free speech: citizens had no such right.[23] What Geneva had safeguarded, and softened for eighteenth-century use, was the right of its citizens to be thoughtful, prosperous Calvinists. For most observers this left ample room for a healthy amount of holiness. It took the clumsy, self-interested manoeuvrings of a man with a much vaster vision to prize apart the comfortably-knit layers of custom, money and theology and to demonstrate that even the city set on a hill could not cope with finding a saint.

23. See Jean Robert Tronchin, *Lettres Ecrites de la Campagne* (Geneva, 1763), p. 10; of course the freedom guaranteed by settling in Geneva was the freedom to profess a Calvinist faith as Jacob Vernet (pastor and professor) pointed out in his *Lettre d'un Citoyen à un autre* (Geneva, 1768), p. 85.

# 'Jam and Jerusalem': Stephen Chivers (1824–1907), Baptist and Village Paternalist

*Michael Booth*

The seeker of a monument to the life, work and genius of Sir Christopher Wren might justifiably be directed towards St Paul's Cathedral; there indeed, *Si monumentum requiris, circumspice*. To a lesser degree, but with equal justification, certain buildings within the village of Histon, three miles to the north of Cambridge, stand as tribute to the life, work and interests of Stephen Chivers (1824–1907). Chivers was a man of parts, market gardener turned jam manufacturer, philanthropist and founder of the Histon Baptist Church, constructing over many years a profitable business and a network of influence, both in local commerce and in Baptist affairs. From the buildings he constructed, from the Baptist Church Book, from oral evidence and from the articles written by loyal Chivers's employees in his firm's house magazine, it is possible to put together a biography of the man. Reading this material, much of it uncritical and fulsome in its praise, it is hard not to feel that what one is reading is purest hagiography. Chivers was not a 'saint', though he was sincerely religious: he was a shrewd businessman, economically ambitious, to whom religion gave the ultimate sanction.

Stephen Chivers was born in Histon, the son of a small market gardener. The family came from the neighbouring village of Cottenham during the eighteenth century but, come their prosperity towards the end of the nineteenth century, Huguenot ancestry was claimed. P.H. Reaney has confirmed the French origin of the surname, from Chièvre, meaning 'she-goat', denoting someone of agility.[1]

1. P.H. Reaney, *A Dictionary of British Surnames* (London: Routledge

The name has also been found among Baptists in Wiltshire, but no connection proved. Chivers was raised as a Wesleyan Methodist and attended Histon's Wesleyan Methodist Church. As a young man, having taken over the running of his father's market garden and thus joining one of the dominant groups within the community, he sought office within the Wesleyan society, serving as steward and taking an interest in the Sabbath School, which numbered 140 scholars in 1853.[2] Expansion of his father's business, brought about by increasing the deliveries of fresh fruit and vegetables to the London market first by road and then, after the 1840s, by rail, made Chivers the chief of Histon's market gardeners. He was ambitious for his church, and came to despise the small and rather plain building which in his opinion did not reflect the growing respectability of its membership. With one of the local preachers, a Cambridge draper named Jacob Wisbey, Chivers pressed for a new chapel. The superintendent minister refused to consider the suggestion, for the chapel had been built with the financial support of a wealthy local family, and the minister had no wish to offend them. Tension mounted during 1857, with the Wesleyans dividing into two camps, the more numerous (but less prosperous) group supporting the minister.

In April 1858 Stephen Chivers and Jacob Wisbey led seventeen others out of the Wesleyan Church, blaming 'certain acts of the "*Ruling Powers*" infringing on their liberties as of the Christian Church...'[3] After some discussion, when it was suggested that the seceders form a Congregational Church, it was decided 'to unite in the Fear of the Lord...' and establish a Particular Baptist Church. In this one sees the hand of Chivers: he had married Rebecca Frohock of Waterbeach, whose grandfather, as senior deacon of the Baptist Church there, had been one of those who had invited Charles Haddon Spurgeon to its pastorate. The subsequent invitation to Spurgeon to preach at the opening of the new Histon Baptist Church that same year, an invitation which was accepted, confirms a personal relationship between the two men. Certainly Chivers had personal

and Kegan Paul, 2nd rev. edn, 1974), p. 71.

2. *Ex. info.*, K. Parsons, 1986.
3. *Histon Church Book, 1858–1908*, (MS).

knowledge of two earlier Baptist Causes in Histon in 1845 and 1850, and James Smith remembered as a boy hearing Spurgeon preach in Histon before the construction of the chapel.[4] The other seventeen seceders, mostly fellow market gardeners and their wives, were content to follow Chivers's lead. The affairs of the new church were initially entrusted to John Keed, minister of the Zion Baptist Church, Cambridge, who began the first Church Book, but it was Jacob Wisbey who became the first official pastor. The construction of the chapel of 1858, a plain rectangular building with classical aspirations, overlooking Histon Green, was left to the members, who gave time and labour to realize the project. Stephen Chivers donated £30 towards the cost; so did his fellow market gardener James Burkett. C.H. Spurgeon gave £27 and Thomas Chivers, Stephen's brother, gave £25. From the outset, the Chiverses determined that this was to be their church.

Under the influence of John Keed of Zion, and perhaps of Spurgeon himself, the new church adopted 'Open Communion' but '*determined* to be cautious in the reception of new Members *admitting* such only as are able to give *Scriptural* Evidences of having been *Born again*...'[5] Open Communion then, but a restricted membership, and those so chosen were to be first examined by existing members appointed by the deacons for that purpose. Stephen Chivers was one of the first three deacons elected to office.

By the 1870s, having held the offices of deacon and Sunday School Superintendent since the church began, Stephen Chivers's position within his church was strong, not least because of a succession of brief pastorates. His business had continued to expand, and his sons William and John had been sent to Bradford to study marketing and retailing at first hand. The younger Chiverses noted that the biggest customers for their father's fruit were local jam manufacturers, and they tried to persuade their father to branch out in this direction. It took the fruit glut of 1873 to convince Stephen Chivers to do so, and the first boiling was made in one of his barns at Impington, the whole process supervised by a cook from Pembroke College.

4. J.S. Chivers, *Histon Baptist Church 1858–1958* (Cambridge, 1958), p. 9.
5. *Histon Church Book*.

Nonconformist connections provided Chivers with a retail outlet at Messrs Hallack and Bond, whose grocer's shop stood in The Petty Cury, Cambridge, and from the outset demand for Chivers's jam was high. The decision was taken to purchase an orchard behind Histon Railway Station, and work began on a factory building, finished in time for the 1875 fruit harvest. It was named The Victoria Works, but this was later changed to The Orchard Factory. At the first jam boiling there had only been about a dozen of Chivers's workers involved, but The Victoria Works was a much bigger venture. By 1885 Chivers employed 150, including coopers, builders and thatchers, as well as carpenters, joiners, engineers, wheelwrights, blacksmiths and labourers.[6] The aim, in the best traditions of Samuel Smiles, was self-sufficiency. As demand for jam increased, so did the need for more fruit and therefore a greater acreage. In 1885 Chivers's farm acreage was 500, by 1914 the firm owned 4,000 acres, and this increased to 8,000 by 1937.[7] As more land was obtained, Messrs Chivers diversified into other areas of farming, including poultry (which helped keep the orchards free from pests), cattle, pigs and horses.

The agricultural depression of the late nineteenth century had little effect on Messrs Chivers. This was partly due to the policy of diversification, introduced by Stephen Chivers and maintained by his sons, partly to a willingness to invest in new ideas and new equipment, and partly to the attitude taken by the management towards its employees. Stephen Chivers believed that his employees should be made to feel parts of a family, and that each had a personal stake in the future of the company. Writing in 1924, Stephen's son John Chivers recalled that 'Thirty-two years ago we introduced into our business the principle of Profit Sharing among the employees; this has developed into a system of co-partnership under which all permanent workers qualify for an actual holding in the Company'.[8] By the standards of the time, The Victoria Works was a well-lit, airy

6. G. Horridge, *The Growth and Development of a Family Firm: Chivers of Histon, 1873–1939* (Cambridge, 1983), p. 9.

7. Horridge, *Growth and Development*, p. 2.

8. *Contact*, News Sheet No. 14, 'Chivers Centenary Number' (1973), p. 10.

place with fans to remove steam generated during the jam-making process. During the winter the factory was heated by a coal-fired system later replaced by an electric one. The factory grounds were tended by a team of gardeners, and were made available to employees during break times. Stephen Chivers introduced a pension scheme around 1895, compulsory for all male employees, several years before Lloyd George's national system became law. Before 1897 the nearest doctor lived in Cambridge, but in that year John Chivers persuaded his father to appoint a company doctor, who would also practise generally in Histon. Dr Aldren Wright, a member of Emmanuel Congregational Church in Cambridge, and a personal friend of John Chivers, took up the post. Industrial medicine was a new concept, but both Stephen and John Chivers saw advantages in being able to prevent illness among their workforce in addition to dealing with accidents.

Stephen Chivers, now appointed senior deacon for life, supported by the rest of his family, many of whom held church office, pressed for the abandonment of the Baptist Chapel of 1858, which was considered too small and unfashionable and, perhaps, not really appropriate for a church so closely associated with such an important local family. There was no opposition, as there had been when Stephen Chivers had made the same demands upon the Wesleyan Church, and in 1900 the new Baptist Church on Station Road was opened. The choice of site is revealing. It stands in the middle of what can only be described as 'Chiverstown', immediately next to Stephen Chivers's house, close to The Victoria Works and Histon Railway Station, and surrounded by the houses built by Stephen Chivers for his workers. There were practical reasons for wanting a larger building: when the first Baptist Church had been built there had been a membership of nineteen, but at the time of the Church Meeting of January 1897 in which Stephen Chivers first raised the issue, there were eighty-two members and a growing congregation, many of whom were Chivers's employees. The new church was built in red brick in the fashionable 'Free Gothic' style to the specifications of the London architects, Messrs George and R. Palmer Baines, who also designed St Andrew's Street Baptist Church in Cambridge, and the total expenditure, which included new Sunday School buildings, came to £4,921. The opening ceremonies were dignified by the presence of J.H. Shakespeare, Secretary of the Baptist Union, and Edwin Gorsuch Gange, President of the Baptist Union in 1897, men of national stature within their denomination.

The Baptist Church of 1858 was bought by Stephen Chivers and turned into The Institute, a meeting place and social centre for Histonians, the venue for Pleasant Sunday Afternoon meetings, where newspapers could be read and hot baths obtained for a few pence. The Institute also housed political meetings for the Liberal Party, of which John Chivers became local chairman.

Education was one of Stephen Chivers's great interests. He recognized from the outset of the Baptist Church in Histon that there was a need to educate young people in Baptist principles, so that they would grow up in the faith and come naturally to the church as adults. His involvement with the Wesleyan Sunday School before the 1858 schism had proved this, and as Baptist Sunday School Superintendent he retained a personal contact with the schools until his death. As an employer, he was also aware of the need to have a literate workforce. In The Institute, a range of self-improving classes was provided for the men and women of Histon to attend, with guest speakers (not all of them on religious topics) arranged by Chivers and his family.

In 1909, two years after Stephen's death, his son John Chivers purchased a large house near the factory called The Firs, where recreation and evening classes for the whole community were established. The family played a great part in the establishment of Impington Village College, the original building of which was designed by Gropius. Though these later ventures were carried out by John Chivers, one can detect the spirit of Stephen Chivers in them.

Stephen Chivers was the last of the nineteen original members of the Baptist Church in Histon. On Monday 24 June 1907 'the whole village was plunged into grief by the announcement that our Senior Deacon Mr Stephen Chivers had been very suddenly called home'.[9] The Church Book dutifully records that 'his wise

9. *Histon Church Book.*

and matured counsels were ever at the disposal of both ministers and members and he was always ready to help on any good work'.[10] The pastor carefully pasted a photographic portrait of Chivers into the Church Book, writing on the opposite page his wish that 'our dear friend had been spared until October 1908 which would have completed 50 years membership of this Church'.[11] Raymond Blathwayt, writing shortly before Chivers's death, felt that

> Old Mr Chivers is an educational and religious force in the village, and, indeed, throughout the whole neighbourhood. It is character, the character of a straight-forward, God-fearing Englishman, which more than anything else has helped to build up this great business.[12]

Many speakers at his funeral testified to his piety, his generosity and his zeal for the well-being of his neighbours, but not all felt like this. Stephen Chivers, though indeed a 'saint' to some, made enemies. There are old people in Histon today who avoid the Baptist Church because of its links with the Chivers family. They feel that in the old days their jobs and their parents' jobs depended upon regular church attendance, and there is still strong resentment. There is a story that some of them, when only children, would turn up at the Baptist Church on Sunday, nominating one of their number to put his head around the door to see if either Stephen Chivers or his son John was there. If not, the children would run off and play instead. The Chivers family would be horrified at this and would deny that their employees were ever placed under such pressures. Stephen Chivers achieved many things for Histon: he built up a business which gave diverse and full-time employment, providing workers with pensions and medical care, comfortable housing, schools, a fire service (originally for the firm but extended to the local community) and even a cemetery. He made his family *the* leading family in Histon, and therefore to be either admired or criticized. There will always be some prepared to do both.

10. *Histon Church Book.*
11. *Histon Church Book.*
12. *Cambridge Independent Newspaper*, undated article, stuck into *Histon Church Book*, 24 June, 1907.

# 'An Optimism of Grace': The Spirituality of Some Wesleyan Kinswomen

*Clyde Binfield*

'His was a typical Victorian family—staunch Methodists, farmers, merchants. Wesleyan ministers and businessmen.'[1] So, what's typical? The subject of that quotation was a Leeds businessman, one man in a section of society whose outworking might be traced from the late eighteenth century to the mid-twentieth. This particular section is English with some Scottish incomers and some imperial outliers. It is middle class—middle to upper middle in gradation rather than middle to lower middle. Its core is professional with a commercial and agricultural penumbra. It is London, Leeds and Lincolnshire, with London understood to embrace the home counties and the south coast as well as the grand suburban sweep from Hampstead round and down to Beckenham. What holds it together is an accumulation of connexion and property. Here are both foresight and Forsytes. This connexion, reinforced by its property, moulded, extended and justified by its education, is announced by its cultural

1. [Virginia Vickers], *Spin a Good Yarn: the story of W. Farrar Vickers* (Leeds, 1978), p. 7. I am indebted to Mr Colin Dews for this reference. This essay is one of three studies in collective, or connexional biography, exploring the Pocock family. This explains why each has the same beginning. The other two explore what might be called the professional and the pastoral cements of the cousinhood. They are C. Binfield, 'Travelling Preachers and Lay Popes: the Case of R.M. MacBrair', *Proceedings of the Wesley Historical Society* 49 (May 1993), pp. 29-43; and 'Architects in Connexion: Four Methodist Generations', in Jane Garnett and Colin Matthew (eds.), *Revival and Religion since 1700. Essays for John Walsh* (London: The Hambledon Press, 1993), pp. 153-81, esp. p. 154.

similarity. Here are people who look like each other, though they may not always like each other; who know each other or at least know of each other; who think like each other even as they react against each other. Their bond is religious.

Such connexion, at least from the Reformation until the last thirty years, was inevitable in English society. It was a consequence of the fragmentation of that English Christianity which remained nonetheless coterminous with English society. Within the past thirty years English Christianity has ceased even notionally to be coterminous with English society and the sort of network here described has largely ceased to exist. The property which made possible an entire way of life has been dissipated by the fiscal policies of successive governments, the education which shaped that way of life has become too diffuse for it to play much part in forming a new connexional culture, the commercial and professional worlds have developed complexities which go far beyond family convenience, and the religious bond has gone.

Our Leeds businessman's 'typical Victorian family', his pride of Pococks, Hills, Vickerses, McAulays, Dawsons, Shillingtons, Harts, Archbutts, was confessionally Evangelical, denominationally Wesleyan. Its religious loyalty was marked by connexional responsibility, expressed in a recognizable spirituality and thence refined into a recognized culture. Its weekday boots were not easily separated from its Sunday shoes. These architects, property developers, accountants, solicitors, doctors, farmers, oilmen and brokers, not to mention ministers, here a JP, there a high sheriff, here the master of a livery company, there a padre, here a saint (though sinners all), there a black sheep, would have led significantly different professional lives had they not been Wesleyan Methodists.

This essay's concern is with what cements this cousinhood and justifies its collective biography: its connexional spirituality, and particularly its female dimension. It was the women of the connexion who breathed life into it. Their spiritual character breaks out of the obituary prose, deepens the affectionate constraints of familial memoirs, survives unrestrained in occasional journals and commonplace books.

The connexional Methodism began with the sixteen-year-old

Hannah Fuller's conversion in 1770. A devout and persistent little woman, sixty years a Methodist ('she may have been thought by some to suffer her zeal to overcome her prudence'), she persuaded her betrothed, William Pocock (1750–1835) to attend Methodist meetings. This was in High Wycombe but they settled in London, where William turned successively from master carpenter to cabinet maker to builder, sporadically prosperous and uniformly respected as each of these. Their Methodist loyalty lay in City Road. There Hannah 'found her way to the early services...for several years by help of a penny candle'.[2] Come prosperity and suburban life in Leyton it was Hannah who made a Methodist chapel the precondition of her removal. There Wesley visited them.[3] Thus began the male Pococks' traditionary life of connexional responsibility and cumulative office-bearing.

In the third generation this was concentrated in the strenuously practical pieties of the two Pocock brothers, William Willmer (1813–1899) and Thomas Willmer (1817–1889), one an architect, the other a surgeon, one in Wandsworth, the other in Virginia Water. Thomas's wife had been a Congregationalist 'of the older and, as many think, the better school. To the end she retained more than a little of the original stamp of her training.'[4] William's wife, however, was Wesleyan born, bossy and quick and brimful of frustrations, 'her assistance...eagerly sought in those Church works then understood to be within the range of female exertion, a range much more circumscribed than at present':[5]

2. W.W. Pocock, *In Memoriam William Fuller Pocock FRIBA, 1779–1849* (priv. 1883), pp. 39, 9.

3. Pocock, *In Memoriam*, p. 9.

4. She was Elizabeth Rose Seth Smith (1816–1883) the Belgravia builder's daughter. 'Memoir of Mr Thomas Willmer Pocock', *Wesleyan Methodist Magazine* (January, 1892), p. 4. I am indebted to the Revd. K.B. Garlick for this reference.

5. She was Sophia Archbutt (1815–1889). 'Memorial Sketch of Mrs W.W. Pocock, of Wandsworth'. *The Christian Minister* (12 June, 1889), p. 810. I am indebted to the Revd K.B. Garlick for this reference.

## The Pococks

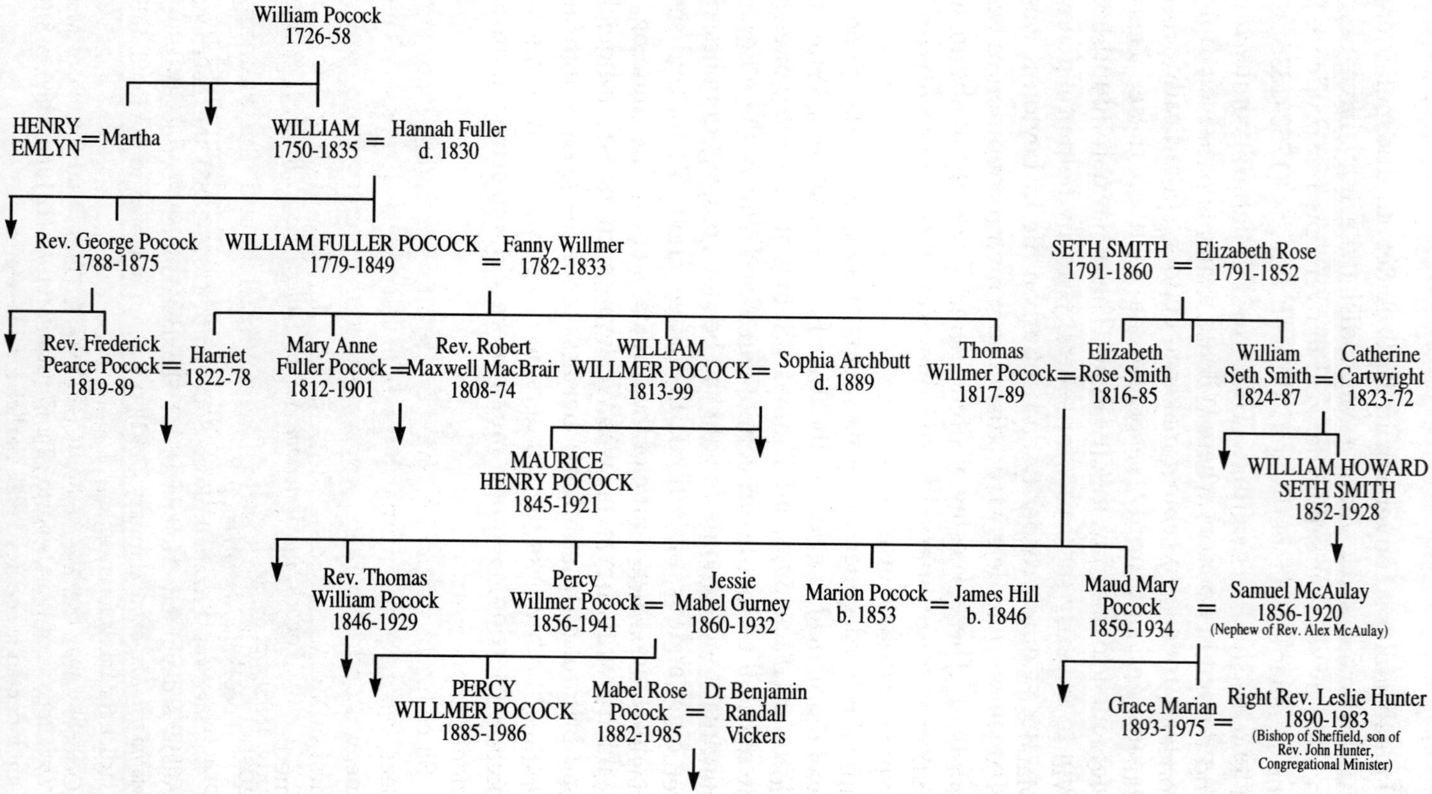
William Pocock
1726-58
HENRY EMLYN = Martha
WILLIAM 1750-1835 = Hannah Fuller d. 1830
Rev. George Pocock 1788-1875
WILLIAM FULLER POCOCK 1779-1849 = Fanny Willmer 1782-1833
SETH SMITH 1791-1860 = Elizabeth Rose 1791-1852
Rev. Frederick Pearce Pocock 1819-89 = Harriet 1822-78
Mary Anne Fuller Pocock 1812-1901 = Rev. Robert Maxwell MacBrair 1808-74
WILLIAM WILLMER POCOCK 1813-99 = Sophia Archbutt d. 1889
Thomas Willmer Pocock 1817-89 = Elizabeth Rose Smith 1816-85
William Seth Smith 1824-87 = Catherine Cartwright 1823-72
MAURICE HENRY POCOCK 1845-1921
WILLIAM HOWARD SETH SMITH 1852-1928
Rev. Thomas William Pocock 1846-1929
Percy Willmer Pocock 1856-1941 = Jessie Mabel Gurney 1860-1932
Marion Pocock b. 1853 = James Hill b. 1846
Maud Mary Pocock 1859-1934 = Samuel McAulay 1856-1920
(Nephew of Rev. Alex McAulay)
PERCY WILLMER POCOCK 1885-1986
Mabel Rose Pocock 1882-1985 = Dr Benjamin Randall Vickers
Grace Marian 1893-1975 = Right Rev. Leslie Hunter 1890-1983
(Bishop of Sheffield, son of Rev. John Hunter, Congregational Minister)

> She was a woman of striking personality, strong mind and will, a meet help-mate for her husband whose idiosyncrasies she understood perfectly, and influenced. Strangers did not always see her best side; but Mrs Pocock was a truly good woman...[6]

It is with two sisters-in-law of the next generation, however, and the mother-in-law of one of them, that this paper is chiefly concerned. Maud Mary Pocock (1859–1936) was the youngest daughter of the Thomas Pococks of Virginia Water. Jessie Mabel Pocock (1860–1932) was married to Maud's next brother, Percy William Pocock (1856–1941) of Egham. Jane Annie McAulay was Maud's mother-in-law.

'Maud's religion', recalled her daughter Grace, 'never lost the marks of reality, fervour and simplicity which characterize authentic Methodism'.[7] Those marks were the proof of personal experience. Educated to recognize her potential, Maud determined to make her way professionally in the world, for hers was the first generation of women for whom such determination was sensible. But she was thwarted by illness and deflected by marriage. The illness became chronic, forcing on her such a stewardship of energy as had characterized her invalid father's retirement in Virginia Water. The marriage was a country marriage, transporting her bodily to different routines and other ways. It brought her increasing material prosperity until the years of conservative discipline could issue in a comfortable liberation, personal but not selfish, open to inspired whim and the occasional extravagance of 'that other gift long ago of "the ointment of spikenard very costly"'.[8]

Since her health and stamina barred nursing and service overseas, Maud's determination was to become a dispenser. This meant London in 1886, 'towny air' and the undermining rigours first of Methodist community life on Clapham Road and then of medical women's hostel life in Bloomsbury. It was the world of gospel temperance, street evangelization and the daunting practicalities of mass do-goodery, incessantly disciplined by a lessening of self. It was the Methodist London of Hugh and

6. 'Death of Mr William Willmer Pocock, B.A.', *Methodist Recorder* (October, 1899). Cutting in possession of Mrs R. Dunk.
7. [Grace Hunter], *Maud Mary McAulay: A Memoir* (1939), p. 11.
8. Hunter, *Memoir*, p. 101.

Katherine Price Hughes and Mark Guy Pearse and their determination to harness all sorts in mission, not least 'ladies of leisure, culture, refinement and devotion...for this most blessed work'.[9] Maud Pocock was such a lady and, though teased by a rich (Congregational) uncle that she was really husband-hunting, she faced her chosen life unblinkingly:

> I am trying to get up a S. London cabmen's tea for 600 and their wives, about 1,000 altogether and mean to get a sheep and some potatoes out of Uncle Charles to pay him back. The men and women will get a service first and then have a cram of meat and potatoes and coffee and tea. Jolly. We shall have it in our Hall...I've been to Paris for 4 days with Mrs Meredith. We went to see the Missions.[10]

Maud's was a temperament made for Paris. But though Europe opened to her in old age, in youth it was temperance and soul-work ruefully detailed for her missionary brother in South Africa:

> Last night we had a temperance lecture by a Rev. Pyper of Belfast entitled Bible wines. Its only effect on me was to create a great thirst for sparkling Moselle and vow after this my first experience that attendance at such lectures would be few and far between. It was feeble. I can understand your Temperance Cause is mighty and needs real firm upholding but to those who have no temptation—and only take wine occasionally—what is the good of propounding arguments by the million which all seem insufficient to *me*, and to call the Bible a Total Abstinence book is below its dignity. I can't swallow a great deal I hear amongst my good people.[11]

Removed to what she called 'spinster chambers' in Hampstead, equidistant from another rich (Anglican) uncle and a pleasant 'Methody Chapel', she continued cheerfully to unburden herself to her brother Tom:

> I hear the Salvation Army in the distance. People can't say London is not evangelized. There's a story going of a poor

9. West London Mission Annual Report (1890), p. 7 quoted in P.S. Bagwell, *Outcast London: A Christian Response* (1987), p. 25.

10. Maud Pocock to the Revd T.W. Pocock, 143 Clapham Road, 2 December 1886: Hunter, *Memoir*, p. 22.

11. Hunter, *Memoir*, pp. 22-23.

> woman who had five different lady visitors one morning. Each asked to pray and to the latter's request the poor woman acquiesced if she might go on with her washing the while![12]

Maud too acquiesced. She took the discipline, but she would not join the discipline:

> It will come all right in the end. I am only a Boarder at Clapham. I won't join them. A Miss Jennings of Hanbury is Sister Sophy and looks after our food at 143 Clapham Road but only has a limited supply of money to do it withal. My pride has to bow for I may only enter the dining room where she sits by *knocking* and at meal times!!...They hoped to have me Sister Maud by now but not so! They are very good I would say naught against them, but they are small...[13]

Her health, her father's last illness and then her marriage with its rapid consequence of three children in three years took Maud from the pressures of South London sisterhood to those of Lincolnshire country life and the unsought discipline of a prolonged debility which drew upon all her spiritual resources. Her daughter analysed that discipline: Bible as bedrock, constant prayer as inspiration, and for tools a sequence of apparently random jottings in note books or on the backs of envelopes:

> Her imagination roamed the world, the suffering, the outcast, nations and peoples in distress, and came back to the fish packers in Grimsby, or animals on the farm, or the peculiar needs of people who live on barges. She accumulated large masses of the simpler forms of religious books, pamphlets, tracts and cards, such as are anathema to the highbrow. Some she herself found helpful for the same reason that she liked to read the *Children's Newspaper* rather than *The Times*; a great deal of it she gave away, having always near her heart the needs of simple people. There was, however, nothing sentimental about her religion. It drew balance and dignity from the Bible. In the spiritual life her standards and values were taken from the austere vision of Old Testament prophet and psalmist and the sacrificial faith of the writers of the New Testament. In these her mind was soaked and she turned naturally to them for guidance.[14]

12. Hampstead, 12 May 1887; Hunter, *Memoir*, pp. 24-25.
13. Hunter, *Memoir*, p. 23.
14. Hunter, *Memoir*, p. 99.

When Maud Pocock of Glenridge, Virginia Water, married Samuel McAulay (1856–1920) of Aylesby, her London assurance met a Lincolnshire practicality leavened by the same quality of spirituality. Maud's mother-in-law, Jane Annie McAulay, was at once a gentleman farmer's daughter and a Wesleyan minister's wife in whom culture met piety with irresistible charm as she set her elder son on right paths for public life in a farming county, keeping the ancestral Methodism anxiously bright for this young man of the 1880s:

> I sometimes have a fear...that your young friends may lead you further from Christ instead of nearer to Him. You know that you have not many religious young friends whom you love and admire much (I mean young gentlemen friends)...
>
> We have had such an interesting letter from Francis telling us that after earnest prayer, the peace of God came into his heart, so that he could not doubt that he was a child of God. This was when he returned to rest March 1st. Our first and best wish for all our beloved children is that they may have the love of God dwelling in them.
>
> While I like my children to be discriminating hearers of the Gospel, I do *not* like them to be critical hearers. As it is your lot often to hear local preachers, sometimes poor ones, pass over without notice any mistakes of grammar or pronunciation, and gather all the honey that you can from every sermon or prayer. It would be a great comfort to us if you cultivated a love and respect for Methodism, her *preachers* both travelling and local and all her peculiar privileges, etc., etc., as if you should get the Aylesby farm, it would be a great joy if also you filled your dear Grandfather's place as to Methodism in some sort...[15]

Samuel did get the Aylesby farm and as Justice of the Peace, Deputy Lieutenant and High Sheriff he more than filled his grandfather's place, held to it by his mother's Methodism with its sensitive apprehension of service and eternity and sound living:

> *Pray* about everything.
> Don't, darling, say 'Hang it' and such things and don't let Francis.
> It is more *manly* to avoid slang than to use it.[16]

15. 10 February 1878: Hunter, *Memoir*, p. 44.
16. 30 September 1880: Hunter, *Memoir*, p. 46.

Six years later the concern was for Sunday observance:

> It gives me many an anxious feeling because we do not as a family (I speak for myself as well as for the rest) spend the Sabbath day as well as we did when you were children...There is so much laxity now abroad in so many ways that it troubles me much. May we all as a family be thorough (*not half-hearted* Christians).[17]

And inevitably there was a concern for right Bible reading, which elicited from the granddaughter who used these letters for a family memoir the surprised admiration of one liberated by Girton College and the Student Christian Movement for its demonstration of 'how spiritual sense triumphed over a belief in verbal inspiration':

> Do you read the Scriptures straight through every word? I do—your father, too, says he thinks it the best method. Thus when you are reading those portions less profitable, take the New Testament at the same time, or take one book of the Old Testament straight through, then one of the New, alternately; and the more you read the Scriptures thoughtfully and prayerfully, the more you will delight in them. And though it is a simple habit, it is a very helpful one to learn one verse of Scripture every Sabbath and repeat it every night the following week before you go to sleep. You would thus get a good store of Scripture in your mind—and some day you would be so glad that you have done it.[18]

Between his mother and his wife Samuel McAulay of Aylesby was set firm in Wesleyan ways. The best assessment of the context upon which London Pococks and Lincolnshire McAulays alike worked came from the next generation. At Cambridge as a student and in SCM as a travelling secretary Maud's daughter, Grace (1893–1975), extended the tradition before leaving it when she married Leslie Hunter, an Anglican priest though a Congregational minister's son. She wrote about it just as her husband became Bishop of Sheffield. Bishop Hunter's churchmanship defies accurate description: neither Catholic nor Evangelical, yet both; too firm to be Broad but beyond all things *national*. He developed as deep a sense of a national church as

17. From Grimsby, 23 August 1886: Hunter, *Memoir*, p. 46.
18. From Scarborough, 27 September 1884: Hunter, *Memoir*, p. 47.

his wife retained an instinctive sense of that church's no less national counterpart:

> Sam and Maud had a very real reverence for the Established Church but their churchmanship was centred in Methodism and they would never yield to the constant pressure of those who thought of Methodism as a kind of frill to real Church membership. In those days the Church of England still bred intolerance of dissent, and its failure, particularly in country places, to recognize and appreciate the church life of Methodism often divided village life where a greater charity might have found a way of cooperation. No one who has lived even for a time near the heart of the village Methodism of that generation could fail to be impressed by its fruits. Local preachers might at times be hard to bear and extemporary prayers at the prayer meeting were not all on the same spiritual level, but it brought to simple people an articulateness and a sense of reality about the facts of religion which brought richness and warmth into their lives, and gave them a simple culture of their own. They knew, too, how to appreciate the best types of Methodist sermon which met their desire for knowledge as well as for grace; and if the minister had the sense not to omit the long words but to explain them, so much the better.[19]

Of the Methodist women so far described, Hannah (Fuller) Pocock's was the closest to that experience but Sophia (Archbutt) Pocock, Maud (Pocock) McAulay and Grace (McAulay) Hunter were all nurtured within its discipline. They mediated its values from one generation to the next and from one household to another.

Maud's wedding had been muted by the aftermath of her father's death, the weather and the approaching dispersal of the family home. Even so the chapel was 'pretty and quite full', with the child attendants in cream and white and bronze and Mark Guy Pearse to conduct the ceremony. Maud's sister-in-law Jessie was not impressed by him. He took the service 'so abruptly and so very quickly that it all seemed over in a few minutes. The Exhortation he left out entirely, so that to me the service seemed very poor.' Maud drove off in showers of rain, '*very* nice in her grey dress and jacket and black hat' leaving a

19. Hunter, *Memoir*, p. 57.

depleted household: 'We all had fine fun them—supper in the dear old Dining room and great jokes...':

> And now the sweet old home...is all stripped and vacant! The furniture is divided and the house is empty. It seems very strange and weird when we go up there and I really do not care to go... Some day I trust we shall all meet as '*unbroken families*' in the 'Happy Land, far far away'.
>
> Yes! The children were singing that sweet hymn tonight and after it as I undressed them I asked them which part of today [Sunday] they had enjoyed most and Mabel said 'The Sunday School' and Willmer 'Chapel'![20]

Thus described, breathless with the delights of barely contained sentiment, the high points of home life seem pleasantly unremarkable. Yet the proprietary love for a chapel as snug as home and the sense of responsibility to and for a community whose core is family should be savoured. For here is due order without hierarchy, the Methodist family of faith naturally building up the family connexion, one sister despatched lovingly to Lincolnshire, another to Leeds. Jessie Pocock's own wedding day ('so calm and bright and beautiful just the very day for a wedding')[21] had been nine years earlier. Jessie was just twenty-one (her birthday 'so bright and sunshiny in every way').[22] Hers was a South London suburban wedding (from Hurstleigh, Clapham Park), and 'all the dear old cottagers round had turned out to have a look and gave us a good cheer'. There were the bride's uncle to officiate, five bridesmaids including Maud, 'some good singing and the hymns printed', and a honeymoon in Scotland, not forgetting 'the wonderful Cross at Iona'. And so to Egham and 'our own dear little *home*!!' with its two servants and 'most important of all—coming to know each other':[23]

> They were happy weeks but writing all this four years after our marriage I can say that these weeks and all the weeks now are far, far happier than that first year and I would not go back to it again for anything.

20. Jessie Mabel Pocock, Journal 1881–1910, MS, 4 June 1890. In possession of Mrs R. Dunk.
21. MS Journal, 28 July 1881.
22. MS Journal, 1 July 1881.
23. MS Journal, 28 July 1881.

That was a rare note for Jessie's journal to strike but it sets the perspective for what might otherwise seem an over-easy moralizing. Jessie Pocock's faithful moralizing, like Maud McAulay's envelope-back jotting, was drawn from a constant engagement with the bereavement and prostration chronically incidental to large families (Grace reflected that Maud's generation of Pococks had at least sixty cousins.[24] Jessie cannot have been far behind)—terminal illness long drawn-out, wedding upon wedding, the birth of children:

> Dear little *Emily Maud* was born at twenty past six in the morning (Friday) I have so much to thank God for; restored health, help given at a time sorely needed and His strength and comfort through all. My dear old nurse, Mrs Tiffin, came the day before, so that everything was ready and only waiting for the little stranger. All seemed ordered in a wonderful way and as I sat by the fire in my pretty room where so many important events had taken place, I felt it so and could thank God from my heart and claim His help to the end. Percy fetched the Doctor at 5 a.m. and Baby was born at 6.20 a.m. and Percy went off to Manchester for the night on the three minutes to eight train that morning.
>
> Maud had written up over my mantel-piece some lines of Browning:-
>
> 'Herself so just a type of womanhood
> That God saw fit to trust her with the holy
> task
> Of giving life in turn'
>
> They seemed to be engraved on my mind all through that night with a pen of iron, though when all was over I saw what a 'holy task' had been committed to me and how humbled and unworthy I should feel.
>
> Baby is very very small, dark hair, blue eyes but strong. The day after her birth dear Marion was taken very ill and for the past month she and I were both led aside from the busy world to lie still and be patient and to listen in the quiet to the voice of God. Now we are both restored to health again, and oh how much we owe him.[25]

Jessie's background was Evangelically diverse. Her father was one of the parliamentary shorthand-writing Gurneys. They

24. Hunter, *Memoir*, p. 10.
25. MS Journal, 11 February 1887.

shared a distant common ancestry with the Quaker banking Gurneys of Norwich but their particular stock was Baptist and the uncle who married Jessie was a past-President of the Baptist Union and principal of the Baptist Regent's Park College, Joseph Angus. One branch had become Evangelical Anglicans: John Hampden Gurney the hymnwriter and Russell Gurney the lawyer belonged to this branch. Others married into Quakerism—Gilletts and Dixons. Wherever women Gurneys married their surname tended to follow them: Gurney Smith, Gurney Salter, Gurney Angus, Gurney Dixon, Gurney Fordham, Gurney Masterman, Gurney Pocock. In Jessie's immediate family, her brother Tom (1856–1929) became an Anglican clergyman and her own formation, at least since her father's death when she was only three years old, was Wesleyan.[26] Evangelical piety was thus the dominant motif of the huge cousinhood of which she was part. She took her Methodist version of it with the utmost seriousness, using her journal to record her leadings:

> I want this book to be a memorandum of events and also a book of thoughts, a second Mrs Kitty Trevelyan [*sic*]. When I am sad and weary and lonely I shall come and tell this book all about it and make it my friend when I am alone.[27]

She began her journal on her wedding day with a retrospective glance at the three years since she had left school. 'My life since then has been such a wonderful leading of God that I must recount it in this book'. From the first she mingled thought and event:

26. See W.B. Gurney, *Some Particulars of the Lives of William Brodie Gurney and his Immediate Ancestors* (priv. London, 1902). For Joseph Angus (1816–1902), John Hampden Gurney (1802–1852), Russell Gurney (1804–1878) see *Dictionary of National Biography*.

27. MS Journal, 28 July 1881. Mrs Kitty Trevylyan was the creation of Elizabeth Rundle Charles (1828–1896) whose hymn 'Never further than Thy Cross/Never higher than Thy feet' is still sometimes sung. For all her early Tractarianism, her *Chronicles of the Schönberg-Cotta Family* (1862), a story of the times of Luther, ensured her a firm Nonconformist following. So did *Diary of Mrs Kitty Trevylyan: A Story of the times of Whitefield and the Wesleys* (1865).

> my spare time I filled up by visiting my dear old women. I always shall believe that those dear old persons were sent me in answer to prayer; for when I left school I prayed that I might have some work in the vineyard and then Annie Dean told me of the poor creatures. There were three of them. Mrs Ault, Mrs Smith and Mrs Crook. The first was my special charge and many a sum I collected to keep the old lady. She told me once I was like a little mother to her, and indeed I got to love her so much. My dear Percy helped me many a time in connexion with these old women; on one occasion he and I visited old Mrs Smith together to present her with a large-print, nicely bound Wesley Hymn Book.
>
> About nine months were spent like this and then came an event which altered the whole course of my life.[28]

Jessie was school-sick. She yearned for her old school, Laleham, and its headmistress, Miss Pipe.[29] She wished to return. 'I somehow could not feel quite happy about it. God had planned out my home life for me so plainly that it was vain for me to hope Laleham could be the right path for me.' She went to talk to Miss Pipe 'but providentially she would not be home for two hours [.] I determined to stay at home and to make myself more contented'. Three days later Percy Pocock proposed to her. 'I had loved him for two years...and after a week of thought and prayer I accepted him.' Two months later Jessie and her brother Tom stayed at the Pococks' Glenridge for the first time, only to

28. MS Journal, 28 July 1881.

29. For Laleham and Miss Pipe see C. Binfield, *Belmont's Portias: Victorian Nonconformists and Middle-Class Education for Girls* (Dr Williams's Trust, 1981), pp. 19-25; Anna M. Stoddard, *Life and Letters of Hannah E. Pipe* (1908), and the description of Fox How, 'a well-known girls' school not a hundred miles from London—so called in memory of Dr Arnold, according to whose principles the school was founded and carried on' in the novel by the Wesleyan authoress, Ellen Thorneycroft Fowler, *The Farringdons* (1900), pp. 51-62:

> It would be futile to attempt to relate the history of Elizabeth Farringdon without telling in some measure what her school-days did for her; and it would be equally futile to endeavour to convey to the uninitiated any idea of what that particular school meant—and still means—to all its daughters.
>
> When Elizabeth had left her girlhood far behind her, the mere mention of the name, Fox How, never failed to send thrills all through her, as *God Save the Queen* and *Home, Sweet Home* have a knack of doing...

be called back to Hurstleigh: their mother was dead. The switchback of Providence was not to be gainsaid and Jessie, who could not bear to find it ignored, noted down a shocking instance of such ignoring. It was what an acquaintance in King's Lynn told her:

> he had been very dangerously ill, and when ill he sent for a clergyman and told him he was anxious about his soul and could not rest until he felt sure he was saved. The clergyman's reply was—'You are depressed and low; you must go about and try and get strong and then these fears will not trouble you!' Such a reply indeed! Oh that these clergymen—God's under-Shepherds...may be converted *themselves* before they try to help others.[30]

Illness and death caught at her old women and her old school-friends and her new chapel friends quite impartially:

> My dear old woman, Mrs Ault, died. I was told of her illness in Chapel and went at once to her; and when I spoke to her and asked her if she remembered me she replied 'Miss Gurney, oh *yes*!' with such a beam. She was ill only two or three days and then my charge was taken from me to a place where she would be everlastingly cared for.[31]

Ten years later it was Jessie's cousin, 'Poor dear Nellie Dudeney', her life story one of those tragedies inevitable to every family though its details have a poignancy peculiar to Victorian middle-class women. There but for the grace of God and social coincidence went so many of them:

> She had only been ill since June, gradually getting weaker and growing worse and on the second she died quite peacefully and ready to go. I wrote to her on New Year's Eve but I hear she was too ill to read my letter though she looked at my card.
>
> It is a great disappointment to me not to have seen her lately but God knows best. I left it with Him praying that if it was right for me to go and see her the way might be opened but the chance never came. One thing after another hindered it so that I could only send messages. It is a sad ending of a short lonely life. Since 1882 she has had to earn her own living and this she did for some time as mother's help; then later on she took to Hospital Nursing

30. MS Journal, 28 July 1881.
31. MS Journal, 28 July 1881.

which was a great delight to her. At the Ventnor Consumptive Hospital she became engaged to a Dr Williams and was looking forward to being married in about a year's time. Instead of that consumption developed itself in June, which Nellie believes she distinctly *caught* from a patient at Ventnor, and now she is gone. She was buried at Ore Cemetery on the 4th January. Dear Little Nell! *Poor* no longer lonely no longer but happy for evermore; for

> They who with their leader
> Have conquered in the fight
> For ever and for ever
> are clad in robes of white.[32]

Late that February a 'dear, dear friend', Emmie Milsom, followed:

> She wrote me a sweet letter at the end of January saying she had to undergo a serious operation but she looked forward to it quite hopefully and spoke of the time when she would be out in the fresh air again, little thinking it would be the fresh air of Heaven.
>
> The operation was performed on Thursday the twentieth and in the afternoon she began to sink under it and on Sunday evening at 8.20 p.m. she died. I cannot believe that my dear friend Emmie is gone, so faithful, so loving, so true. I had no idea until I lost her *how much* I loved her. The world will always be more empty without her and I cannot bear to think of that sweet little home without her.
>
> We parted at the gate of this house and she told me to come and see her after Tommy was born and I said 'I may not be alive' and she said 'Jessie *I* may go first' and that was the last time we met. Darling Emmie! Thank God I ever knew you! And thank Him for your deep loving friendship, so true at all times. I feel so sorry that I have not been to see her oftener, we seem to have given up much for our children and now I regret not seeing my darling, little, delicate Emmie. Farewell sweet one! In Heaven we shall meet again.[33]

Illness and swift eternity were drawn wonderingly from God's plan by this young woman in her early thirties. In 1884 she endured one prolonged prostration and a second followed in the summer of 1892. Percy had returned from family business in Canada, sorting out the aftermath of a brother's tragedy.[34]

32. MS Journal, 2 January 1890.
33. MS Journal, 23 February 1890.
34. Percy Pocock was a solicitor but his practice was largely confined to

> He noticed at once that I was ill. The next morning Dr Giffard came up to see him and they had a long talk, the outcome of which was that I was ordered away to the Highlands for six weeks. My dear friend Mrs Beattie came to tea with me and to say goodbye the day before I started and little indeed did I think that she would never enter my house again! Dear, dear friend! I am the better for having known you and sore is my heart that the friendship is so suddenly cut short and the dear friend sinking into eternity![35]

Jessie's destination, for which 'special daily strength was granted', was the Hydro at Crieff, one of those Victorian palaces catering for the health and holidays of the serious middle classes for whom spas were too lively and sanatoria not yet invented;

> Life there was simply delightful; 260 staying in the Hydro and yet it was so beautifully managed that there was no muddle. In the morning we had breakfast at 8.30, then came Prayers with a delightful hymn, then the morning letters and then a stroll...along the Cinder Path, where we would find a shaded corner and lie down under the trees...Our old friends from Streatham Hill, the Dawsons, were there also and poor Mrs Dawson never returned home. They had all been to Lina Glen driving one day and Mrs Dawson took cold which was followed by pleurisy and she died in a few days at the Hydro.[36]

Early next year Mrs Beattie died too. 'Such a quiet beautiful death—just like her life—she said goodnight to all her girls and then asked, "Any messages?" and fell asleep and died'.[37]

The Dawsons were family connexions: Cousin Sophie Pocock had married a Dawson. Mrs Beattie was a chapel friend, like Emmie Milsom. Chapel entwined with home to promote high thoughts and discipline the spiritual life. The year's end, time for watchnight and covenant, was ever suggestive. The watchnight for 1881 was at Brixton Hill, the chapel very full, five young people in the Gurney pew—Jessie and her Percy, Tom and his Annie from Barnes ('a dear Christian girl'), and Emily who never married. There were beautiful addresses from Mr Sharr

the legal and property affairs of his extended family.

35. MS Journal, 5 July 1892.
36. MS Journal, 20 July 1892.
37. MS Journal, 28 February 1893.

the circuit minister, and the great Dr Punshon: 'a memorable service it was'.[38] Thereafter Jessie's base was in Egham. 'Another year gone and the first Sunday in a new one!' She wrote on 2 January 1887:

> We have all had many mercies to praise God for during the old year, and now as the New Year opens I consecrate my life afresh to God. I sorely need His strength and grace; there is much, very much to try me in my own heart's failings, in doubts and fears about the future and in daily cares and worries: but I feel that His grace *has* been sufficient for many and I pray that I may be taught to draw from it more constantly and effectually. I feel that I am but a 'poor cumberer of the ground'—no fruit borne for the Master's glory during the old year and my time may soon be over and the great eternity commenced! May He help me to trust Him more fully so long as I am spared and to live in Him more entirely. I want to be taught to be more like Mary and less of the 'Martha'—to leave all in His Hands and to have more of the sweet rest which comes from doing so.[39]

The following year saw them once more at Brixton Hill, 'a lovely Sunday...such a treat and the Watchnight service was beautiful. Mr Sharr conducted it and preached on "What is your life? It is even as a vapour etc."' Mr Sharr was of particular help at that time. His Sunday morning sermon was strong in the Methodist tradition, its theme was 'The very God of peace sanctify you wholly and I pray God your whole spirit, soul and body be *preserved blameless* etc.' That service too was beautiful.[40] Jessie was ready for the new year:

> In the afternoon we had a most beautiful Covenant Service and I felt it was a great blessing to me. Mr Sharr is so earnest and so devout that the whole service seems to feel the influence. With God's grace I will do better this year and bring forth more fruits to His glory. I feel that the old year was full of failure and sin—so full that I cannot bear to think of it but God will help me to keep the Covenant I have made for as Mr Sharr said—'He who hath saved will *keep*' and I believe it and will trust Him. This year seems all uncertain—we go out not knowing whither but God will guide us.

38. MS Journal, written in July 1881. For William Morley Punshon (1824–1881), see *Dictionary of National Biography*. He died in April 1881.

39. MS Journal, 2 January 1887.

40. MS Journal, 29 December 1887.

'I would rather walk in the dark with God
Than walk alone in the light'

We only pray that He may lead us to a place where we may work for Him and prosper in soul.[41]

Jessie's uncertainty was that of moving house. In June 1888 the Percy Willmer Pococks left Remington Villa, cement-rendered on Egham Hill, for The Chestnuts, redbrick and new on Egham Hill:

> The last Sunday evening in the dear old home, where seven happy years have been spent! This week we are leaving it and our future is in God's hands. I can hardly believe it and yet now that the time has come there seems so much to be done and thought of that there is very little time for sentiment and regret. In this sweet home we began our married life; in this house our three dear children were born; since we lived here Percy's dear Mother has been taken away; my dear brother Tom has become a clergyman and married; Marion has been married...We have much to praise God for; especially for health. Not once has any one of us been seriously ill (unless it was myself) and our children have grown up and developed in health and strength.
>
> Then we praise God for the spiritual good which we have received in the seven years. He has taught us many lessons and we have got to know many dear Christian friends. He has been with us through all our cares and of course we have had cares—the greatest have been caused by servants and by constant misunderstandings and motives misinterpreted.
>
> I mourn tonight that I have done so little for God in the seven years—so little compared with what I *meant* to do and all has been so poorly done and full of self. Oh may He forgive me and baptize me afresh and make me a blessing to my Society class and Sunday School class!...Farewell sweet little home! Farewell happy years! They will soon be gone and gone for ever![42]

Three months later Jessie was praising God with jubilee sighs of relief at the spaciousness of The Chestnuts:

> May God bless our home and make it a rich blessing to very many. Oh that I could give up my will to Him and really leave all things in His Hand and believe that He *does* know best. This is my great difficulty and the future must be met and what but His strength can do it?

41. MS Journal, 1 January 1888.
42. MS Journal, 17 June 1888.

> 'What but Thy grace can foil the tempter's
> power
> Who but My Guide and stay can be
> In cloud and sunshine oh *abide with me.*'[43]

Jessie was three months pregnant at the time of the move and her fourth child, Thomas Gurney Pocock (1889–1967) was born two days before Christmas. Naturally the Christmas story 'came to me with fresh light and deeper meaning than ever before', and the sound of her older children playing with their old nurse delighted her:[44]

> I am so thankful for it all and now I can calmly and thankfully look into the future and feel that
>
> 'He who has fed *will* feed
> He who has led *will* lead'
>
> I am sorry that I have not trusted God more in the past. He has always been more to me than all my expectations and I fear that I must have grieved Him by my doubts.

Five weeks later Jessie went

> to our dear Chapel to return thanks. My heart was very full and I have so much to praise for. We had such a lovely service and 850 for the closing Hymn. My dear girls and class members gave me such a welcome and the student prayed so beautifully for me.[45]

Jessie's journal was both a conversation with God and an *aide-memoire* for one. In July 1890, 'the loveliest holiday I have ever had in my life' was preceded by a Channel crossing of classic proportions, rain pouring down and waves

> dashing right over the ship and falling down into the cabins. but I did not feel afraid. I thought of my dear girls praying for us and of Jesus walking on the sea and stilling the Tempest and I felt His power was the same as of old and was happy.[46]

More domestic storms with another sort of crossing were pondered in November 1891:

43. MS Journal, 9 September 1888.
44. MS Journal, 23 September 1888.
45. MS Journal, but clearly written later.
46. MS Journal, 16 July 1890.

> My dear old Nanna left us after living here for four years and four months. It seems all changes and partings and this one has been to me a very sad one. I am so thankful for all she has done for our children and especially for her *Christian* influence over them. I wish she and I could have agreed better, but all that was forgiven before we parted and I look forward to meeting her in Heaven where we shall thoroughly understand each other and be able to talk and sympathise, in the presence of our common Lord and Saviour Jesus Christ.[47]

Jessie Pocock's temperament met with the Methodist holiness tradition and was spiritually formed by it. In 1893, however, she experienced the further spiritual dimension for which her temperament yearned. She described it in her journal in May 1894.

> *Outwardly* things have been going on in much the same way—'new mercies each returning day'—our children growing, Percy in better health and so on. But the change I want to write about this time is an internal one—a glorious one with no sadness in it but *rest* and *peace*. Just a year ago we all went down to Littlehampton for five weeks and during that time I attended one of dear Mr Sargeant's Holiness Conventions...It opened my eyes and I saw that God had not got *full* possession of me but that there were things in me not quite given up to Him; and I let it all go and He took me to be fully His. I hardly know how to explain it all but oh! the difference it has made in my life. He leads me now moment by moment, bearing my cares for me, speaking to me constantly by His Holy Spirit and helping me to live literally with
>
> 'Nothing between Lord!
> Nothing between!'
>
> This year has had more peace in it than ever before and I do *praise* God for this revelation.[48]

The Littlehampton Convention became a fixed point of Jessie's year. Such things were spiritual hydropathy for the middle classes, no doubt, but here nonetheless was the cure for which her spirituality was preparing her, as any reading of her journal makes clear. The Keswick movement and its many by-products, of which Littlehampton was one, provided for Jessie's generation of Evangelicals what Methodist holiness had offered an

47. MS Journal, 22 November 1891.
48. MS Journal, 25 May 1894.

earlier generation and what the Oxford Group would offer the next two generations, an uncluttered certainty which allowed for action while setting it free of anxiety or guilt. It liberated middle-class Protestants from their constant anguish at the immensity of the impossible; and it enabled them to accept the limitations of mortality. Jessie wrote about this later at a point of special stress:

> The whole of this year was one of very great financial anxiety. Things had been getting more and more anxious during 1904—investments bringing in nothing, houses un-let, cotton gin seeming failure and so on all round. We were in sore straits and wondered if God wanted us to leave our own pretty home. At the beginning of 1905 we gave up a servant and in various ways tried to re-trench. But anxieties only thickened until we were in a great way as to the next step and could not see God's hand leading us. In addition to this my poor Percy's health was beginning to give way with the strain. The yearly Convention at Littlehampton was just gathering and we seemed led to send a special request for prayer in this time of anxiety. The prayer was read out and offered on a Sunday and a great peace and assurance seemed to come over us that the prayer had been heard.
>
> Two days later came the answer in a most unexpected way. A gentleman wired to know if we would let our home furnished at once for 2 months!
>
> It was all very wonderful and in a few days we had packed up and were off—my dear boy Willmer to stay with various friends and the rest of us to go about and shift for ourselves for 2 months. Emily was *most* kind to us exceptionally so, befriending us and making us feel at home in her home. The rest and change of it all were very nice and the visits to Cambridge and Margate and if it had not been for the anxiety and suspense through which we were passing the holiday would have been enjoyable. As it is looking back on the time, I think of it with *great* thankfulness for God's deliverance and pray that never again may we go through such a time of anxiety and heartache. We returned home in July and in August.[49]

Life on Egham Hill, whether in Remington Villa or its grander successors, The Chestnuts and The Beeches, as refracted in Jessie Pocock's journal, was entirely domestic. Chapel was part of that domesticity; indeed the Egham chapel had largely been

49. MS Journal, May 1905.

built by assorted Pococks. Eternity too was domestic, that eternity which cared for old Mrs Ault and allowed for heart-to-heart chats with Nanna. So too were the lives of their neighbours beyond the Great Park. In June 1897 Jessie accompanied Percy to London for the Queen's Diamond Jubilee procession:

> It was a very wonderful sight and one never to be forgotten—the vast crowds all kept in perfect order, the numberless soldiers and pageantry and then *least* but by far the most imposing sight of all the dear old Queen, bowing and smiling in her gracious and *lovely* way.[50]

The new century brought a double dose of the inevitable yet inconceivable, to be domesticated and moralized. The first was in January 1901:

> Our dear Queen is dead! What news to have to write in this book! Our dear, noble beautiful Queen, who has been to us all a Friend and sympathizer besides being a Queen, gone for ever! I heard she was ill on Friday evening, day after day the bulletins were more serious and on Tuesday evening at 6.30 she died. What an example she has left.[51]

The second followed in June 1902:

> Our dear King was to be crowned on the 21st and great was the joy and excitement all over England. We felt it would be a sight our children might never see again, so we were very glad when the Scrivens wrote and invited us all up to their London office to see the Procession. Then we arranged for them all to come here from school and as the time grew nearer and nearer we all became more and more excited and looked forward most eagerly to the great and happy day. Henry came here from Cambridge and brought with him his friend, Mr Taylor.
>
> The day before the Coronation I went up with Adie Crosby to see the decorations and to meet Emily at the Royal Academy. It was an ideal day, warm and bright and everyone seemed happy and in the highest of spirits. London was full of visitors, English and foreign: dear boys and girls were pouring in by all the trains from school ready for the next day and it made you feel as if you wanted to keep singing or humming all the time so happy it all was.

50. MS Journal, 21 June 1897, written on 10 June 1900.
51. MS Journal, 22 January 1901.

> I joined Emily at the Academy and we walked round looking at the Pictures for an hour, when suddenly a gloom came over the whole place. People stopped talking and began looking from one to another in an anxious, frightened way. A lady came up to me and said—'Excuse me, but could you tell me if this is true about the King?' There was mystery over everything and we felt we must go out and find what it all meant. Alas! We soon knew, for as we came into the street all the newspaper boys were calling out 'Coronation Postponed—Serious illness of the King'. Yes, the dear King was dangerously ill and an operation was needed *at once* if his precious life was to be spared. I can never forget the *return* journey to Egham that day with its tremendous contrast. Everyone was subdued, some were crying quietly, others were disappointed in a more selfish way because their hopes of a holiday had been dashed to the ground—in fact *every* thing seemed suddenly changed, and where there had been all happiness and joy before, it was now all gloom and sadness.
>
> Then followed anxious days of watching and it was with very deep thankfulness that we came out of this with our dear King spared to us—a better man for the suffering and endeared to his people in a way he could never have been without it. Truly it was the Hand of God from beginning to end and looking back now we can see that
>
> 'All is right that seems most wrong
> If it be His sweet will'[52]

With the old Queen's death and the new King's illness and recovery we return to the male Methodist world of connexional office and overseas responsibility. Henry from Cambridge was a South African nephew of Percy's, and something of a black sheep. Both Jessie and Percy had brothers in South Africa. Sam and Maud had a beloved uncle who died in South Africa. Another Pocock brother settled in Canada. In the next generation there were missionaries in China and India. Domestic horizons were imperial horizons and missionary lore added a geographical dimension to the eternity mulled over by the drawing-room firesides of Glenridge and Aylesby and The Chestnuts. No family with kinsfolk in South Africa, and few families living near Aldershot, could view the soldiers of the Queen in a purely ceremonial light. Nor was that in the Pocock tradition. Military-readiness was increasingly in tension with

52. MS Journal, June 1902.

soul-readiness for these Methodists. Their women expressed both readinesses in nursing.

Jessie Pocock was fortunate in her health, family, education and material circumstances. That does not diminish the anguish in her soul or its aspiration. Neither does it make its spiritual expression less representative. Hers is the authentic voice of ordinary Evangelicalism, unremarkable enough for it to escape the attentions of ecclesiastical or feminist historians. Yet the unremarkable must occasionally be remarked upon especially if it is phrased in the consistent accents of Wesleyan wives and mothers holding the faith and their families in Connexion with an unquenchable optimism of Grace.

# A Spark in North East Asia: A Personal Hagiography of a Scottish Missionary to Manchuria: John Ross (1842–1915)

*James H. Grayson*

## I

Although the *Oxford English Dictionary* simply defines 'hagiography' as 'the writing of the lives of saints',[1] the American *Merriam-Webster Dictionary* gives the further definition of hagiography as an 'idealizing or idolizing biography'.[2] This second definition is closer to the common use of the word, which is to single out a work as being an unreliable source because events and statements are so distorted as to emphasize a particular spiritual or ideological quality in the life of the individual there described. In short, 'hagiography' is now a term of disparagement. This is to be regretted because if, as the *Merriam-Webster Dictionary* also states, hagiography is a 'biography of saints or venerated persons', hagiographical writings should be a prime source of information about certain historical figures. The problem with biographical writing in this vein is that because the person has been selected to illustrate certain virtues or qualities, the tendency will be, or has been, to idealize all of that person's qualities or actions. Yet there is no reason why hagiographical writing should not be a good source of historical information provided that the writer has taken a

1. *The Shorter Oxford English Dictionary on Historical Principles* (Oxford: Clarendon Press, 3rd edn, 1973), p. 913.

2. *The Merriam-Webster Dictionary* (New York: Pocket Books, 1974), p. 320.

critical stance towards his subject, who should be described as a believable or real person. This definition, of course, sets aside the question of whether or not exaggerated hagiographies tell us something of the intellectual and religious climate of the time of their writing, irrespective of their accuracy about the facts of the subject's life.

This essay is a personal hagiography, that is to say, it is a biography of a Scottish missionary for whom I have come to have the highest regard. In writing this personal hagiography, it is my hope that the figure whom I describe will be a believable human being with faults as well as virtues, and that his life will illustrate some of the positive qualities of Christian missionaries in China during the nineteenth century.

While I was working on a comparison of the transmission of Buddhism and Christianity to Korea, I came across a Scottish missionary to Manchuria, Dr John Ross (1842–1915), who had been intimately involved with the translation of the New Testament into Korean. I became fascinated with his character, and decided to write a Korean-language biography of his life as part of the centennial commemoration of the Korean translation of the Bible.[3]

There are three principal sources of information about John Ross: first, oral information, derived either from the recollections of older people living in Ross's home village of Balintore in Ross-shire known to his descendants; second, letters written by Ross to the United Presbyterian Church of Scotland mission board office in Edinburgh and published as part of a missionary journal, *The United Presbyterian Missionary Record* and its successors; and third, correspondence largely from the mission board in Edinburgh to Dr Ross in Manchuria which is now in the archives of the National Library of Scotland in Edinburgh.

As far as I know, there survives no diary written by Ross. He

3. Kim Chŏng-hyŏn (James H. Grayson), *Na Yohan: Han'gug-ŭi ch'ŏt sŏn'gyo-sa* (John Ross: Korea's First Missionary) (Taegu: Kyemyŏng University Press, 1982). See also James H. Grayson, 'The Manchurian Connection: The Life and Work of the Rev. Dr John Ross', in J.E. Hoare, Chong-hwa Chung, *Korean–British Relations, Yesterday, Today and Tomorrow* (Seoul: Korea University Press, and Chŏngju: Cheongju University Press, 1984).

did, apparently, keep a diary, because mention of it is made at several points in *The United Presbyterian Missionary Record* and other sources. I presume it to have been lost in the Sino-Japanese War of 1894–1895, or the Boxer Rebellion of 1900, or the Russo-Japanese War of 1904–1905, when his home was destroyed or vandalized.

The information in this essay on the early life of Dr Ross comes almost entirely from the recollections of older members of his home village in northeastern Scotland, supplemented by information gleaned from the records of the local churches. For the story of his life and work in Manchuria, I have relied largely on *The United Presbyterian Missionary Record*. In these monthly reports, one can derive a fairly clear idea of Ross's movements, what concerned him as a missionary, and the sense he had of his missionary vocation. Also the tone of his writings in comparison with the tone of those of some of his colleagues gives a further insight into his broad-minded character. This has been supplemented by the letters held by the National Library of Scotland. This correspondence is useful because it gives a clear indication of the difference between the understanding of China and of mission to China held by the mission board in Edinburgh and that held by 'the man on the spot'.

## II

John Ross was born on 9 August, 1842, the eldest son of Hugh Ross, a tailor in the village of Balintore in eastern Ross-shire, Scotland. Raised in this village as a native speaker of Gaelic, Ross first learned English when he went to school. He proceeded from school to the Theological College of the United Presbyterian Church of Scotland in Edinburgh, completing his studies in the mid-1860s. As he was a native speaker of Gaelic, the church was eager to assign him to the Gaelic-speaking churches which even in those days were suffering from a lack of clerical supervision in the native tongue of the members of the congregations. Ross, on the other hand, felt the tug of a missionary calling and hoped to be sent out to India. In the end, he served as a Gaelic-speaking minister for six years in Inverness, Portree on the Isle of Skye, and Stornoway in the Outer

Hebrides. By the early 1870s, he was able to convince the church authorities to send him out as a missionary. In late April 1872, Ross and his bride of one month left Scotland for Chihfou (Cheefoo) on the Shandong Peninsula of China.[4]

Although now little known even by missiologists and church historians, John Ross must stand as a significant figure in the history of Christian missions in China during the latter part of the nineteenth century. There are eight reasons why his role in the transmission and development of Christianity in China can be seen as important: John Ross was effectively the Father of the Protestant Church in Manchuria and Korea; he translated the New Testament for the first time into the Korean language; he was an important force in the early stages of the ecumenical movement amongst the missionaries in China; he founded and directed the first theological college in Manchuria; he was a linguist of considerable ability and accomplishment; he was a pioneer in the study of the Korean language; he was a pioneer in the study of the history of Manchuria and of Korea; and he was an original thinker about the origin and nature of Chinese religion and history.

This essay provides a discussion of these points in illustration of Ross's claims to greater recognition in the development of Christianity in China.

*Ross: Father of the Manchurian and Korean Churches*

The first Protestant missionary to Manchuria was the peripatetic missionary of the Presbyterian Church of England, William Chalmers Burns (1815–1868). His deathbed call in 1868 for the evangelization of Manchuria was answered by the Presbyterian Church of Ireland which sent two missionaries to the treaty port of Yingkou at the mouth of the strategic Liao River. John

4. Grayson, 'Manchurian Connection', pp. 19-23. The conflict which Ross felt between missionary service and pastoral work in the Gaelic-speaking areas of Scotland was resolved in early 1872. In a letter dated 2 February 1872, Dr William McGill, Secretary of the Foreign Mission Board of the United Presbyterian Church of Scotland reminded Ross that it was 'better to be a mission spark than a flame in Easter Ross' (in the Archives of the United Presbyterian Church held in the National Library of Scotland in Edinburgh). Ross had no questions about his vocation after this.

Ross arrived in Chihfou on 23 August 1872 and was strongly advised by the representative of the National Bible Society of Scotland, Alexander Williamson (1829–1890), who was also in charge of the United Presbyterian mission in that area, to cross immediately to Manchuria before winter set in and the Pohai Sea froze up. Ross did so, becoming the fourth Protestant missionary to Manchuria.[5]

Although John Ross was not the first Protestant missionary to Manchuria, he was clearly the most energetic and the one who had the clearest idea of a missionary strategy and a plan for the development of a mission there. Although his two Irish colleagues left Manchuria before the close of the decade, his own continued presence was subsequently augmented by the arrival of his sister Catherine, together with John McIntyre (1837–1905), who was to become his brother-in-law, and others. Ross saw very early on that for the mission to prosper it had to do two things. First, it must develop a band of native Christians who would be the actual evangelists, and second it must establish its headquarters in the Manchurian capital, Mukden (modern Shenyang), which was also nominally the second city of the Chinese Empire. Both of these aims were achieved well before the close of the 1870s.[6]

In reading the reports which Ross wrote throughout this period, it becomes obvious that he had a very systematic approach to the work of evangelism. Rather than leaping immediately from the treaty port of Yingkou to the capital city, Christian communities were started in all the towns along the main road to Mukden. Thus, by the close of the 1870s, there was a string of Christian groups throughout the heartland of southern Manchuria. Ross's method of evangelization is interesting also because he eschewed the widespread and indiscriminate dissemination of tracts, and street-evangelism. Rather, following an ancient Chinese precedent, he set up a discussion hall where people were invited to come and hear Christianity propounded and debated. He invited his hearers to argue with him about questions of ultimate religious interest. Records of these sessions show that even in the 1870s, when he

5. Grayson, 'Manchurian Connection', pp. 23-25.
6. Grayson, 'Manchurian Connection', pp. 23-25.

was quite a young man, Ross had a profound knowledge of Confucian classical works. Missionary statistics from the early part of the present century also show that, proportionate to the population, the Manchurian mission was one of the largest and most successful in China. This is undoubtedly due to the facts that Dr Ross early on had a plan for the development of the mission, that he had a profound knowledge and acceptance of Chinese culture, and that he relied primarily on Chinese converts themselves to be the principal Christian evangelists.[7]

Alexander Williamson had one other influence on John Ross. During a visit to William Chalmers Burns, Williamson had taken the opportunity to go to the *Kaoli-mên* (known to Europeans as the Corean Gate), the principal customs barrier between Ch'ing China and Chosŏn Korea. Williamson was excited about the possibilities for evangelism in Korea, should that closed 'Hermit Kingdom' ever open up. He discussed the possibilities for the development of a mission to Korea with John Ross before he set off to Manchuria in late 1872. By October 1874 Ross had made the first of two trips to the Corean Gate, at a time when it was open for a market to which Korean merchants could come across the border legally and enter into Chinese territory. Ross was looking for someone who would be willing to act as a Korean language tutor. Although unsuccessful on this first trip in obtaining a language tutor, the incident points up the fact that within two years of his arrival in Manchuria Ross had already conceived a plan to translate the New Testament into Korean and to disseminate it as a 'silent missionary' within that 'Hermit Kingdom' where no foreigner was permitted to enter.[8]

During his second trip in April 1876, Ross obtained the services of an educated merchant of herbal medicines, Yi Ung-ch'an, who agreed to teach Ross the Korean language and to help in the translation of the Scriptures. The translation of the New Testament began in 1877, the first translated books of the New Testament were published separately in 1882, and the entire New Testament was published as a single book in 1887. This was the only complete translation of the New Testament

7. John Ross, 'The Chinese Missionary Problem', in *The Missionary Review of the World* 3.12 (1890), pp. 901-907.

8. Kim Chŏng-hyŏn, *Na-Yohan*, pp. 28-29.

until 1906. By the time that missionaries first arrived in the Korean peninsula in 1885, there were already established communities of Christians in the northeast, in the capital, Seoul, and amongst the Korean communities on the northern side of the Yalu River in Manchuria itself.[9]

*Ross: Translator of the Korean New Testament*

To Korean Christians, Ross's greatest contribution is that he directed the translation of the New Testament into Korean. This project reflected two basic missionary concepts advocated by him. First there was the belief that local people were the most effective evangelists because they knew and understood the cultural and social context better than any foreigner could, and secondly there was the belief that for instruction in basic Christianity it was sufficient to translate the Bible and to allow the local Christians to read and make up their minds on the various religious questions which might arise. John Ross's views on the method of dealing with the question of concubinage and ancestor rituals, which were major moral and religious issues facing nineteenth-century missionaries, provides a revealing contrast with the methods of his contemporary James Hudson Taylor (1832–1905).[10]

Ross began the process of translating Scripture by studying the Korean language through a Chinese language textbook which he had written, *Mandarin Primer* (1875). His study of the Korean language began in 1876 and resulted in the first Korean language textbook in a Western language, the *Corean Primer* (1877). As Yi Ung-ch'an, Ross's tutor, had invited friends of his from the Korean city of Uiju on the Yalu River to come to Mukden, Ross was able to gather together a translation team by the late 1870s which took up residence in his home in Mukden. Ross acted as supervisor and director of this team, assisted by his brother-in-law, John McIntyre. The team, whose

9. Kim Chŏng-hyŏn, *Na-Yohan*, pp. 31-32.

10. John Ross, 'Corean New Testament', in *Chinese Recorder and Missionary Journal* 14 (1883), November–December, pp. 491-97. See also Ross's remarks in James Johnston, *Report of the Centenary Conference on the Protestant Missions of the World Held in Exeter Hall (June 9th–19th) London, 1888* (London: James Nisbet and Co., 2 vols., 1888), II, pp. 62-63, 96-97, 387-88.

membership varied over the years, worked according to a fixed routine and submitted work daily to Ross—and during Ross's absence to McIntyre—for comment. The translation was done several times, at least four times and possibly more. The first and second translations were a rendering of the Delegates' Version (1850) of the Chinese Bible into colloquial Korean. The third and fourth translations were based on the Greek text. Preliminary drafts of the four Gospels, the Acts of the Apostles, and the Epistle to the Romans were complete by 1879. When Ross went on furlough to Britain in that year, he hoped for financial support for publication from one of the British Bible societies.[11]

Apart from the decision to translate the New Testament, Ross made two further decisions about the nature of the translation which have had far-reaching effects. One was to have the translation put into the Korean alphabet rather than Chinese characters, and the other was the choice of certain key theological terms. The Korean alphabet, now known as Han'gŭl, is a scientific, phonetic script of twenty-four letters by which even a moderately educated person would be able to read the Bible. In Korea, traditional education had meant knowledge of Chinese characters and knowledge of the Confucian classical writings. Consequently, the indigenous script, which threatened the authority of the literate *élite*, had been much disparaged by that class and had fallen into virtual disuse. The Bible was the first major book in a long time to be written entirely in the Korean alphabet. Thus the appearance of the New Testament in Han'gŭl and its wide dissemination led to the revival of the use of the alphabet. Today Han'gŭl is seen as a symbol of Korean nationalism and has a national holiday set aside to commemorate its creation.[12]

11. John Ross, 'Corean New Testament'. See also Kim Chŏng-hyŏn, *Na Yohan*, pp. 35-37.

12. J.H. Grayson, 'Korean Writing System', in R.E. Asher (ed.), *Encyclopedia of Language and Linguistics* (Oxford: Pergamon Press, 1994), IV, p. 1873.

*Ross: Early Ecumenist*

Ross was an ecumenist long before that word gained popularity in church circles. It should be remembered that both the Ecumenical Movement and the World Council of Churches owe their origins to the work and attitudes of nineteenth-century missionaries. In this regard, Ross was typical of many missionaries. Early on, Ross's writings show that he felt strongly that the Irish and Scottish missions should work together to build up a united Protestant church in Manchuria rather than one built on a European denominational model. This united mission could then work to create an effective Chinese church. By 1887, Ross had reached an agreement with the Irish Presbyterian mission as to the boundaries of their respective areas of work. By 1891, the two missions acted in concert to form a single presbytery for Manchuria, the Kuandong Presbytery, which meant that effectively the 'mission' had ceased to exist and that there was now on Manchurian soil a self-governing ecclesiastical body with its own leadership.[13]

Ross had ecumenical interests beyond Manchuria and envisaged a united church for the whole of China. To that end, he participated in many convocations which looked towards the merging of all the denominational mission bodies into a single Chinese church. He attended discussions on church union in 1904 and 1905, and participated in the work of preparing a proposal for church union which was presented to the Shanghai Missionary Conference of 1908.[14]

*Ross: Theological Educator*

Central to Ross's missionary thinking was the idea that Christianity would only spread throughout Chinese society if the Chinese themselves were the principal evangelists and missionaries. Having established a body of Chinese evangelists and created numerous Christian communities in southern Manchuria during the 1870s and early 1880s, Ross instituted a formal programme of theological education for the laity from 1887. Its aim was to produce a theologically sophisticated leadership for the Chinese church. This clearly reflected Ross's feeling that it was

13. Kim Chŏng-hyŏn, *Na Yohan*, pp. 45-46.
14. Kim Chŏng-hyŏn, *Na Yohan*, pp. 65-66.

the Chinese who should propagate and lead the church in their country.[15]

Although the evangelism, preaching and conduct of worship was in the hands of Chinese evangelists, it was only on 14 July 1896 that the first Chinese was ordained to the Presbyterian ministry. To redress the lack of proper theological training for the formal ministry, Ross founded a theological college in the autumn of 1898, and remained its principal for many years. Students were expected to present a high school diploma or its equivalent for admission to the college. For those who could not do so, a special examination tested the competence of the applicant. Ross's work not only reflected the Scottish emphasis on an educated clergy, but illustrated the importance which he laid on the quality of the Chinese leadership. It further demonstrated that Ross wanted to remain on the sidelines in the actual upbuilding of the church and its administration, and was able easily and successfully to adjust to changes in the nature of mission and the situation of the Chinese church.[16]

*Ross: Missionary Linguist*

John Ross was a linguist of no mean accomplishment. It is clear that he had a thorough linguistic or speaking knowledge of eleven languages: Gaelic, English, Hebrew, Greek, Latin, German, French, written Chinese, spoken Mandarin Chinese, Manchu, and Korean. Of these Ross was fluent in four: Gaelic, English, Mandarin, and Manchu. I believe that because he had been bilingual at an early age, Ross did not find the acquisition of more exotic languages to be difficult. He certainly felt at home in each of his languages. There is a story still told in Balintore about an incident after Ross's retirement in 1910 and his return to his home village. Ross was talking one day to some Gaelic-speaking crofters who were looking most perplexed. Ross's son, who was standing next to his father, nudged Ross and told him that he had been speaking Chinese. To be unaware of whether he was speaking in his native language or in a 'foreign' language is a high compliment to Ross's fluency in

15. Kim Chŏng-hyŏn, *Na Yohan*, p. 58.
16. Kim Chŏng-hyŏn, *Na Yohan*, p. 58.

Chinese. Such knowledge of several widely different languages made Ross a sensitive Bible translator whose choice of terms and concepts has withstood the test of time and use.[17]

*Ross: Pioneer Historian*

Even though Ross's missionary accounts show that he was fully occupied with the practical daily matters of mission work, including frequent travel throughout Manchuria, he maintained a lively academic interest in Chinese history and religion. Using Chinese sources exclusively, Ross wrote a two-volume history of northeast Asia, the first volume entitled *History of Corea, Ancient and Modern* (1879), and the second *The Manchus or the Reigning Dynasty of China* (1880). Ross contended that one could not understand either Chinese or Korean history without having a solid knowledge of Manchurian history and affairs. This would seem to be a truism, yet it is a point often overlooked in historical research on East Asia. Ross's history of Korea was the first Western language history of Korea and it is notable for its use of Chinese material rather than the Japanese sources used by William Elliot Griffis (1843–1928) in his *Corea: The Hermit Nation* (1882).[18]

Ross's later work included contributions to the Chinese Bible commentary, which started in 1897. More significant to the general historian would be two late works which indicate the originality of his mature thinking. In 1909, Ross published *The Original Religion of China* which argues that the earliest form of Chinese religion was a form of primitive monotheism. At a time when the evolution of religion from animistic or pre-animistic beliefs was the academic orthodoxy this was an unusual concept to propound. It was, however, based upon his own thorough reading of the ancient Chinese histories and other works. It is a *tour de force* and effectively argues its point. Ross was not alone in holding such views. Andrew Lang (1844–1912) held many of the same ideas about the primal form of religious belief which he expounded in *The Making of Religion* (1898). I am fairly certain

17. The story was told to me by the local shopkeeper in Balintore, Hugh Ross, 1979.

18. Kim Chŏng-hyŏn, *Na Yohan*, pp. 37-38, 54.

that although their views coincide at many points Ross had never read Lang's book.[19]

Ross's final work, published posthumously, was a discussion of the ethnic roots of the Chinese people, *The Origins of the Chinese People* (1916). Ross felt that the Chinese had been a single people since at least the early proto-historic period, equivalent to the Bronze Age. This point of view, although commonly accepted by the Chinese, was much disputed by contemporary Europeans. Ross derived his ideas on the ethnic origins of the Chinese from his reading of ancient Chinese histories and observations which he made during his long stay in China. Subsequent archaeological research has shown Ross to have been correct in his assumptions.[20]

## III

John Ross was a significant, if now little recalled, figure in the history of missions in East Asia. He was unquestionably the father of the Protestant church in both Manchuria and Korea. His mission method reflected both a realistic approach to evangelism and a sensitivity to the culture of China. His linguistic skills enabled him to write two introductory language textbooks, to translate the New Testament into Korean, and to write commentaries on the Bible in Chinese. His knowledge of Chinese history combined with his originality of thought enabled him to write two seminal works on the origins of Chinese religion and the Chinese people. His writings show him to have been both passionately involved with spreading knowledge of the God he loved and with studying the people amongst whom he lived.

It has been my intention that this should be an essay in hagiography, the description of the life of an exemplary man, a Christian missionary who lived and worked in China during a

19. Kim Chŏng-hyŏn, *Na Yohan*, p. 67.

20. Kim Chŏng-hyŏn, *Na Yohan*, p. 68. For the most authoritative discussion of the archaeology of China, see Kwang-chih Chang, *The Archaeology of Ancient China* (New Haven, CT: Yale University Press, 1963). See especially the introduction which discusses the history of archaeology in China.

critical period of that country's modern history. It is a personal hagiography, my own confrontation with the life of a man whom I have found to be appealing and instructive. I do not argue, in fact could not argue, that John Ross was a perfect man. I can only argue that he was a good man, devoted to the tasks which had been given to him. I would suggest that one of the reasons why we study history, one of the reasons why biographies are written, is to learn moral truths or lessons from the past. Hagiography in the best sense should be a critical appreciation of the lives of religious figures to see what moral lessons might be learned from them. The life of John Ross is instructive to the ordinary Christian, indeed the ordinary enquirer, as well as to the professional missionary.

## THE WRITINGS OF JOHN ROSS, A PARTIAL BIBLIOGRAPHY

*Mandarin Primer* (Shanghai: American Presbyterian Mission Press, 1876).

*Corean Primer* (Shanghai: American Presbyterian Mission Press, 1877).

*Corea, Ancient and Modern: With Description of Manners and Customs, Language and Geography* (Paisley: J. & R. Parlane, 1879).

*The Manchus, or the Reigning Dynasty of China* (Paisley: J. & R. Parlane, 1880).

*Korean Speech with Grammar and Vocabulary* (Shanghai: Kelly and Walsh, 1882).

*Yesu syŏnggyŏng chyŏnsyŏ* (Korean New Testament) (Mukden: Wênkuang Shuyuan, 1887).

*The Original Religion of China* (Edinburgh: Oliphant, Anderson & Ferrier, 1909).

*The Origin of the Chinese People* (Edinburgh: Oliphant, Anderson & Ferrier, 1916).

## Mosley, British Fascism and Religious Imagery: Fascist Hagiography and Political Myth-Making

*Andrew Mitchell*

> Fascism realises the spiritual reality of things. The appeal of Fascism is to the spirit, for it summons men to labour and to sacrifice for something greater than themselves.
>
> Oswald Mosley[1]

> ...the deep incompatibility between Fascism and Christianity...
>
> Adrian Lyttelton[2]

G.L. Mosse has remarked that fascism represented 'a new religion with rites long familiar through centuries of religious observance'.[3] Certainly European fascist movements claimed that their ideology was all-encompassing as it catered for both material and spiritual needs. For many adherents, fascism involved a commitment to a 'higher form' of living which was often portrayed as a crusade against 'evil' (usually associated with liberalism, democracy, the Jews, bourgeois attitudes, communism and the like). In turn, this stand against all forms of 'decadence' strengthened the upper echelons of the fascist hierarchies in their belief that their work was a sacred mission.

1. A. Freeman, *We Fight For Freedom* (London: BUF Publications, 1936), p. 44.
2. A. Lyttelton, *The Seizure of Power: Fascism in Italy 1919–1929* (London, 1973), p. 421.
3. G.L. Mosse, 'Introduction: A General Theory of Fascism', in G.L. Mosse (ed.), *International Fascism: New Thoughts and New Approaches* (London and Beverly Hills, 1979), p. 16.

Thus, the 'fascist élite, those for whom life was sacrifice, devotion and self-denial, liked to imagine themselves as a kind of religious order'.[4]

The pseudo-religious character of fascism was most highly developed in the public 'persona' of the leader. He was transformed into the spiritual symbol of the nation and the saviour of his society. He was the repository of supreme knowledge, morality and discipline. Recent work has shed light on fascism's use of religious imagery to enhance the standing of the leader in Germany and Italy.[5] Ian Kershaw's examination of the 'Hitler Myth' has shown that, before 1933, Nazi propagandists successfully linked Hitler with 'a streak of secular redemptionism soaked in pseudo-religious imagery' and, in power, the Fuhrer's 'mission' to ensure German resurgence 'was blended suggestively with religious renewal'.[6] Similarly, the cult of 'ducismo' was based on the purportedly 'divine' status of Mussolini. The reverence accorded to the 'Duce' knew almost no bounds:

> The high priests of fascism were calling Mussolini 'divine Caesar', another St Francis, our 'spiritual father' and 'sublime redeemer in the Roman heavens'. By order of the party, pronouns referring to him had to be capitalised like those referring to God.[7]

Religious imagery was used to confer legitimacy on fascist political rule. Neither Hitler nor Mussolini embraced Christianity (the Italian leader was an atheist) but both, as skilful populists, were well aware of the importance of religious symbolism and ritual in establishing their leadership and the creed upon which it was based. Personality cults, generously laced with traditional Christian forms, aimed to exploit popular piety and confirm fascism as a new faith. Mussolini's depiction as 'the man sent by God to Italy' became a stock-in-trade of the regime as did his view that fascism constituted a religion because it enabled an individual to transcend selfish concerns by 'raising him to

4. Z. Sternhell, 'Fascist Ideology', in W. Laqueur (ed.), *Fascism: A Reader's Guide* (Harmondsworth: Penguin, 1979), p. 363.

5. See for example I. Kershaw, *The 'Hitler Myth': Image and Reality in the Third Reich* (Oxford, 1987) and D. Mack Smith, *Mussolini* (London, 1981).

6. I. Kershaw, *The 'Hitler Myth'*, pp. 106-107.

7. Mack Smith, *Mussolini*, p. 163.

conscious membership of a spiritual society'.[8] The National Socialist vocabulary also borrowed heavily from the language of Christianity:

> Hitler and Goebbels talked about the 'miracle of belief' (now meaning the Nazi faith), appealed to 'Providence' and were not loath to call *Mein Kampf* the 'sacred book of National Socialism'. Indeed, the Fuhrer's closest companions were called his 'apostles', while he himself was often referred to as the 'saviour'.[9]

The myth of the omniscient fascist leader was most apparent in Germany and Italy where it became institutionalized as an integral part of the political apparatus of the State. On a much smaller scale, Oswald Mosley, leader of the British Union of Fascists (BUF), was given a sacred status by his own coterie. This particular canonization can be examined most clearly in A.K. Chesterton's biography of Mosley, *Portrait of a Leader*.[10] Chesterton's book, of course, had several functions. Primarily, it attempted to construe Mosley's political journey from his status as an accepted parliamentarian to his role as a fascist outsider as both logical and consistent. Secondly the author sought to rebut the establishment's view that Mosley was an unprincipled careerist chiefly interested in promoting himself, a sentiment neatly summed up by Stanley Baldwin's comment that 'Tom Mosley is a cad and a wrong 'un and they will find it out'.[11] On a more general level, *Portrait of a Leader* presented Mosley's fascism as an authentic 'British' response to perceived national problems rather than as a foreign political import. Chesterton saw Mosley as a high-minded idealist with an almost religious sense of public obligation, who sacrificed the prospect of high office in party politics in his quest to overcome the forces of corruption and decay in British society. Mosley's portrayal as a spiritual figure has reinforced the claim that the BUF leader was a man of destiny and has contributed much to our

8. B. Mussolini, *The Doctrine of Fascism* (Firenze: Vallecchi Editore, 1935), p. 12.

9. G.L. Mosse (ed.), *Nazi Culture: Intellectual, Cultural and Social Life in the Third Reich* (London, 1966), p. 266.

10. A.K. Chesterton, *Portrait of a Leader* (London: Action Press, 1937).

11. T. Jones, *Whitehall Diary* (ed. K. Middlemass; 3 vols., London, 1969), II, p. 195.

understanding of the appeal of British fascist ideology. Small wonder that commentators such as Richard Thurlow have described Chesterton as 'Mosley's hagiographer'.[12]

In many ways, Chesterton was the perfect choice to write the official biography of Britain's most notable fascist. Born in 1899, the son of a mines supervisor, Chesterton spent much of his early life in South Africa, although he attended Berkhamsted School for a time. After serving with the Durban Light Infantry during World War One, he worked as a journalist and editor between 1921 and 1933, first in South Africa and then in England, where he became the senior editor of a Torquay newspaper group. By the early 1930s Chesterton was employed in a public relations capacity at the Shakespeare Memorial Theatre, Straford-upon-Avon. Joining the BUF in November 1933, he was made a full member of the Policy Directorate within a few months and in 1937 became both Director of Publicity Propaganda and the editor of *Blackshirt*. Early the following year, Chesterton switched to editing the other BUF newspaper, *Action*. It was widely recognized that his journalistic background made him 'the BUF's best polemicist'.[13] Chesterton's commitment to the Blackshirt cause also demanded a single-minded dedication from others. The detestation he felt for literal social fascists can be gauged from the fact that, in 1935, he expelled over 300 members in Stoke because they had turned the local branch into a drinking club.

Furthermore, Chesterton's political transition to, and conception of, fascism has to be seen mainly in spiritual terms. Through this process, he came to view Mosley as the embodiment of the ideals he held dear—a fellow warrior who, having survived the carnage of 1914–1918, was unflinching in his resolve to remodel British society in line with the values of the war generation. His harrowing experiences in the First World War (he was awarded the Military Cross for bravery on the Western Front at the age of nineteen) played a crucial part in Chesterton's future espousal of an irrational and emotional strain of fascism. Life in

12. R. Thurlow, *Fascism in Britain: A History 1918–1985* (Oxford, 1987), p. 143.

13. R. Skidelsky, *Oswald Mosley* (London, 1981), p. 344.

the trenches, with its daily round of comradeship, leadership, heroism, fear and horror, crystallized in Chesterton's mind into a classless social model based on service, self-sacrifice and a collective sense of purpose. The war left him unable to relate to, and contemptuous of, those who had not taken part in the conflict. Conversely, Chesterton regarded those who had fought as a special fraternity because their participation had given them access to a 'deeper reality' which remained beyond the grasp of those who had not seen active service. In his estimation, the combatants had passed through a rite of purification which had turned the survivors into new men by purging them of their vanity and selfishness. Chesterton's interpretation implied the existence of higher spiritual forms of explanation which were superior to more traditional empirical and pragmatic approaches. He emerged from the fighting determined to remain loyal to the war generation, convinced that those who had been enlightened by the 'lessons of the trenches' would be able to pursue a moral crusade for national and imperial renewal. However, he became increasingly disillusioned by the desire to return to 'normality', to pre-war practices, at the expense of the nobler ideals which had been disclosed on the field of battle.

Chesterton's inability to come to terms with post-war Britain was compounded in the 1920s by his role as a provincial journalist and drama critic. His retreat from reality took the form of using a 'higher morality', drawn from English drama, literature and poetry, as a yardstick against which to evaluate the outside world. Having gleaned new 'insights' from the writings of Shakespeare, Shaw and Shelley, Chesterton arrived at his own notion of truth and political action. He accepted the 'challenge of attempting to achieve a heightened consciousness through works of great poetry'[14] without realizing that this had serious flaws. By contending that reality could be properly understood solely in metaphysical terms, without reference to empirical methods, Chesterton's analysis of the political scene was often simplistic and misleading. He did not recognize 'that there was

14. D. Baker, 'The making of a British fascist: the case of A.K. Chesterton' (University of Sheffield PhD thesis, 1982), p. 183.

an epistemological gap between metaphysical values as applied to culture and society'.[15]

Organized religion was rejected by Chesterton in the light of his wartime experiences because of the 'smug religiosity which sought to comfort itself for that most shocking slaughter of Youth and seeks to do so still in retrospect'.[16] He described himself as 'largely agnostic'[17] and, although he was prepared to acknowledge the power of God, he believed that since the Kingdom of Heaven could not be comprehended by mortals, their true vocation was to perfect mankind's earthly existence which represented a spiritual act endorsed by divine authority. This task, to Chesterton's mind, was only being undertaken by Mosley and the Blackshirts. It was hardly surprising then that the almost religious admiration Chesterton had for what he saw as the selfless devotion of the BUF leader and fascism's lofty aims, was often expressed in familiar Christian terms:

> For Chesterton, the achievement of self-sacrifice, disinterested service in the cause of the nation and the Empire, and a devotion to duty at all costs, were ways of achieving the 'godlike' in man and in talking of this he unashamedly uses the language of religious devotion.[18]

*Portrait of a Leader*, however, was no simple projection of Chesterton's prejudices and opinions onto Mosley's career. Although Mosley's adoption of fascism was based on his alienation from party politics and his rejection of orthodox economic and political thinking (whereas Chesterton joined the BUF chiefly because of spiritual and cultural impulses), the differences between the two men should not be pushed too far. Mosley has rightly been seen as an 'authoritarian modernizer' who turned to fascism in an attempt to overhaul Britain's economic and political structures, but even Robert Skidelsky, who championed this view, has, in retrospect, conceded that not enough attention has been paid to the romantic and spiritual dimensions of Mosley's public life.[19]

15. Thurlow, *Fascism in Britain*, pp. 42-43.
16. Baker, 'Making of a British fascist', p. 118.
17. Baker, 'Making of a British fascist', p. 120.
18. Baker, 'Making of a British fascist', p. 203.
19. Skidelsky, *Mosley*, p. 15.

Mosley was not a devout man. His mother 'was noted for her firm Christian principles...Her son did not take after her in this respect: like many others brought up in an age of scepticism, Mosley adapted his family's religion to the demands of secular salvation'.[20] Recalling his schooldays at Winchester, he caustically remarked that 'Anything more repulsive to the religious sense than being dragged to morning chapel between early lessons and breakfast is difficult to imagine'.[21] In addition, he doubted whether dreary compulsory services were the best way to engender a respect for religion. Nevertheless, Mosley's fascist revolt against the 'old gangs' did have a less materialistic side. BUF literature stressed that Britain's political and economic decline was inextricably linked to an all-pervading spiritual and cultural malaise which had eroded 'national values'. Religion was conceived as a useful means of instilling politically and morally 'correct' attitudes so that the population could be mobilized to guarantee the success of fascist reforms. A policy of toleration was canvassed as an important component of the future BUF regime but, in return for this 'absolute religious freedom...no political activity under the cloak of religion should be carried on against the State and...no man should use religion as an excuse for evading his duties to his country'.[22] The incorporation of religion into Blackshirt thinking was intended to help create the new 'fascist man', imbued with the values of discipline, loyalty, patriotism and self-sacrifice. Mosley maintained that 'the Fascist conception of citizenship...is in every way compatible with religion'[23] and, from the outset, argued that, philosophically, fascism was a synthesis of Christianity and Nietzsche:

> On the one hand you find in Fascism...taken directly from the Christian conception, the immense vision of service, of self-abnegation, of self sacrifice in the cause of others, in the cause of the world, in the cause of your country...On the other hand you find taken from Nietzschian thought the virility, the challenge to all

20. Skidelsky, *Mosley*, p. 31.
21. O. Mosley, *My Life* (London, 1970), p. 34.
22. Freeman, *We Fight For Freedom*, p. 44.
23. O. Mosley, *The Greater Britain* (London, 1934), p. 51.

> existing things which impede the march of mankind, the absolute negation of the doctrine of surrender; the firm ability to grapple with and overcome all obstructions...[24]

It is also important to remember that Mosley's own temperament and early political career gave him an all but religious self-assurance that he was a potential saviour of British society. Throughout his life, Mosley never lost the 'belief in himself as an almost magically potent political figure'.[25] Nicholas Mosley has pointed out that part of his father's character was concerned with the building of the 'Mosley Legend', virtually at the expense of achieving power. His faith in his self-appointed role as a charismatic hero gave grounds for suspecting that 'there might be something self-immolating' about his public stands.[26] These instincts relating to his own destiny were fortified by his early successes across the conventional political spectrum. His election to parliament on the Conservative, Independent and Labour tickets between 1918 and 1929 fostered the illusion that individual talent outweighed party commitments. Moreover, his capacity to inspire personal devotion and to generate popular approval through electrifying platform oratory also led him to underestimate the institutional nature of modern political support. Mosley formed the impression that the essence of political power was contained in the reaction of large crowds to rousing speeches rather than in traditional party loyalties. Robert Skidelsky has commented shrewdly on Mosley's romantic disregard for the prevailing norms of British political life:

> He came to prefer the theatre of politics to its substance; which is, perhaps, another way of saying that deep down he wanted to be a legend rather than an achiever.[27]

Without doubt, the central motivating influence on Mosley was the First World War. His period of service in the Royal Flying Corps and the trenches made him determined to keep faith with

24. O. Mosley, 'The Philosophy of Fascism' in *Fascist Quarterly* 1.1, January 1935, p. 39.

25. N. Mosley, *Rules of the Game: Sir Oswald and Lady Cynthia Mosley 1896–1933* (London, 1982), p. 172.

26. N. Mosley, *Rules of the Game*, p. 52.

27. R. Skidelsky, 'Great Britain', in S.J. Woolf (ed.), *Fascism in Europe* (London, 1981), p. 262.

the war generation and ensure that their sacrifices had not been made in vain. Mosley became a self-styled spokesman for the 'brotherhood' of servicemen who had seen the horrors of combat at first hand. He felt that only the values and discipline revealed during the war by his comrades-in-arms and the dynamic Lloyd George could create the new Britain. The events of 1914–1918 left Mosley committed to the twin aims of creating a better society for the survivors of the fighting and of preventing another war. Looking back from the vantage point of the 1960s, Mosley stated that 'my whole political life was in a sense predetermined by this almost religious conviction'.[28] In Chesterton's account, the Great War was of immense spiritual significance for Mosley, heralding a type of conversion:

> The war took Mosley by the throat and forced him into an immeasurably more profound conception of life. It made him see the world for the first time as it really was—a bad, stupid place, run by stupid, grasping and sometimes evil old men. It made him rejoice in the valiant spirit of man which transcended every barrier of class and creed and revealed itself in these heroic days as common to all men who were spiritually whole. The splendour of the average of the race came to Mosley as a revelation, and at once he saw the shoddy conspiracy of exploitation and snobbishness whereby the average man was excluded from his heritage in the bad world that had so suddenly burst into flames. Like thousands of other men, he became conscious that more than a war was involved; that in that fierce agony a new world was being forged—a world which one day would become fit for the habitation of ordinary decent human beings. And he saw too, that when the Germans were beaten there would be needed as firm and indomitable leadership to win through to the new world as any leadership exerted on the field of battle.[29]

Invalided out of the services in 1916, Mosley's response was to enter politics in order to contribute to the post-war reconstruction of British society. Mosley regarded himself as a representative of the war generation going to Westminster to secure their rightful inheritance. Initially, he supported Lloyd George because of his vision of a 'land fit for heroes'. Chesterton approvingly quoted the Prime Minister's exhortation:

28. O. Mosley, *My Life*, p. 100.
29. Chesterton, *Portrait*, pp. 18-19.

> Let us cleanse this noble land. Let us cleanse it and make it a temple worthy of the sacrifice which has been made for its honour. Let us cleanse the temple of things which dishonour the structure, dishonour the altar and dishonour the sacrifice made on that altar.[30]

Mosley's new society, envisaged as the enduring monument to the war generation, failed to materialize after 1918, due to international and domestic economic constraints, the downturn of 1920–1921 and the entrenched nature of orthodox financial thinking. Politically speaking, Mosley and Chesterton were either unable or unwilling to reconcile themselves to the realities of post-war British society. The 'money-changers' had not been thrown out of the 'temple' since over half of the 338 Tories who dominated the Coalition were company directors and financiers who had profited from the war. Increasingly, the Conservatives saw a return to the pre-war tenets of party politics as the major objective. Taking his seat as the Conservative MP for Harrow in 1918, Mosley was confronted by 'hard faced men' who did not believe in his mission:

> He saw on every side small dried-up men with mean faces; big pompous pot-bellied men with smug faces; there were thin, spiteful mouths and heavy, selfish mouths; there were yellow skins and flaccid skins; and in almost every eye there was a glint of egotism and greed. These were Mr Lloyd George's soldiers of peace; the men entrusted with the 'cleansing of the temple', the crusaders on behalf of the new age which was to be built upon the agony of youth. Mosley saw them as they were—a Parliament mostly of profiteers and opportunists, assembled not to further the cause of the new world but to patch up and conserve the ugly old world which had brought them great wealth in the past, and which would bring them still greater wealth in the future as long as they retained the reins of power.[31]

This began, in Chesterton's view, a process of growing disillusionment with the mainstream parties which finally led, in the early 1930s, to Mosley's rejection of the liberal-democratic system altogether. Underlying Mosley's shifting political loyalties in this period, it was claimed, was his steadfast commitment to

30. Chesterton, *Portrait*, p. 24.
31. Chesterton, *Portrait*, p. 27.

the establishment of a society which reflected the wartime ideals of social justice and economic betterment. One by one, however, the vehicles for reform within the system were found wanting. By refusing to compromise on the articles of his 'faith', Mosley allegedly exposed bourgeois parliamentary politics as a pious facade.

Under the Coalition, Mosley saw the impetus for post-war reorganization peter out and traditional 'old gang' methods resurface. Gradually, he came to the conclusion that both Lloyd George and the Tories would not implement reform because of their attachment to a parliamentary system which stimulated careerism, placed a premium on retaining power and was heavily influenced by conservative economic interests. In the autumn of 1920, he severed his connection with Lloyd George and became an Independent. With this break, Mosley 'made it clear...that in any choice between expediency and principle he would stand by principle—an intolerable heresy'.[32]

When Mosley joined the Labour Party in 1924, his action was again presented as a model of consistency. Labour's remarkable new recruit justified his turn to the left by arguing that the 'new spirit' of social and economic advancement was strongest in the socialist ranks, adding that it 'is not so much a merely political spirit as a religious one'.[33] Chesterton thought that this epitomized the true nature of Mosley's political motives:

> While all other politicians have been following personal and party advantages, Mosley has looked upon the just and proper ordering of public life as a religious duty as sacred as any obligation which humanity has been called upon to perform...he cut[s] through the murky bourgeois concepts which set so much store on religious appearances while encouraging political and economic practices which are a denial of every true religious impulse.
>
> It is this sense of religious purpose, together with a profound faith in his fellow men that survives every disappointment, which has inspired Mosley through his career and which today makes certain his victory.[34]

32. Chesterton, *Portrait*, p. 32.
33. Chesterton, *Portrait*, p. 48.
34. Chesterton, *Portrait*, p. 49.

Mosley's association with the Labour Party ultimately proved to be another bitter experience. He had assumed that socialism in power would implement far-reaching economic and social reforms. In fact, in government, both Labour and the Tories were committed to economic orthodoxy and 'sound' finance. As Chancellor of the Duchy of Lancaster in 1929–1930, he felt that Labour was in a position to apply bold new policies which, hitherto, had been either ignored or discounted. His expectations were high and his sense of mission obvious:

> Before we leave this mortal scene, we will do something to lift the burdens of those who suffer. Before we go, we will do something great for England. Through and beyond the failure of men and parties, we of the war generation are marching on and we shall march on until our end is achieved and our sacrifice atoned.[35]

He was unable to persuade a conventionally-minded Labour leadership to accept the reflationary Mosley Memorandum as a solution to the mounting unemployment problem and long-term economic decline. A Keynesian-style critique was anathema to the decision-makers in the Cabinet. MacDonald's so-called 'surrender' in the crisis of 1931 hardened Mosley's judgment that, under pressure, socialism would betray its principles and the pledges made to its supporters. In a parting shot, he asked 'What must we think of a Salvation Army which takes to its heels on the Day of Judgement?'[36] Labour's inability to implement radical reform, together with the electoral débâcle of his embryonic New Party, helped to convince Mosley that the liberal-democratic parliamentary system was ineffective and immoral. No longer willing to play by the rules of what he regarded as an outdated game, Mosley was drawn towards the activist politics of the fringe.

Having turned his back on the established political order, Mosley's adherence to fascism, according to Chesterton, could be attributed to the urgent need for a new force in public life which was healthy and unsullied—'a great new movement of new men and new methods—a surging, passionate movement, not of Party-wrangling and expediency-mongering,

35. Skidelsky, *Mosley*, p. 178.
36. O. Mosley, *My Life*, p. 263.

but of spiritual rebirth...an instrument with which the British nation might cut through the tangled undergrowth of decadence...'[37] Chesterton conjured up a nightmare vision of a liberal society that was moribund and virtually beyond redemption. Britain was being slowly strangled, materially and spiritually, by the vested financial interests which were seen to control the political system for their own ends. Slums, malnutrition in the midst of plenty, broken election promises, unemployment on a vast scale and the neglect of the Empire were adduced as evidence of the selfish, uncaring nature of 'financial democracy'. More importantly for Chesterton, this 'contagion' had debased the moral and spiritual values of the nation by encouraging 'the worship of money or the exaltation of decay'.[38] In their drive for quick returns, economic interests had destroyed commercial morality and the idea of value for money. The profit motive had become the new god in a soulless, hollow, bourgeois world more interested in appearances than substance. Alien financiers, through their control of cinema chains, were imposing a 'bastardized Judaic-American pseudo-culture' on the nation.[39] The press sought to maximize its profits by dealing with sensationalism and intrigue rather than the objective reporting of serious issues. Similarly, the arts were obsessed with sickness and decay. They were the preserve of the spiritually 'diseased'. Chesterton's bleak description showed Britain's vitality, inner strength and civilized status under grave threat.

Mosley's remedy for his ailing country was to form the British Union of Fascists (October 1932). This would promote a national renaissance and counteract all forms of decadence. The BUF was idealized as a crusade against the debilitating effects of liberalism which, from a Blackshirt perspective, had been responsible for the economic, political and spiritual decline of Britain. Indeed, Mosley later wrote that the character of a fascist movement 'should be more that of a church than of a political party'.[40] Chesterton's preoccupation with the mystical and

37. Chesterton, *Portrait*, p. 108.
38. Chesterton, *Portrait*, p. 114.
39. Chesterton, *Portrait*, p. 114.
40. N. Mosley, *Beyond the Pale: Sir Oswald Mosley and Family 1933–1980* (London, 1983), p. 87.

moral foundations of fascism enabled him to equate the latter with 'true' Christianity:

> it is the beginning of a new way of life which is also the Christian way of life...It is the first modern recognition of the mystic truth of the Brotherhood of Man and the need to translate this truth in terms of political action. It is the lifting of the barrage in the great spiritual battle for peace on Earth, goodwill towards all men and the lost joy and adventure of life.[41]

Only this new fascist 'religion', it was argued, could save society because it stood outside the discredited party system and refused to compromise with it. Great emphasis was placed on the 'propriety' of the movement because an austere, incorruptible membership would be required to run the future fascist government efficiently. Chesterton saw the BUF as a type of religious sect drawing in the 'spiritually whole' who were inspired by Mosley's example. These were the men and women who would unselfishly serve the cause 'with religious fervour',[42] untainted by the 'democratic gold-digging mentality'.[43] This concept of a higher civilization which offered a deeper spirituality was to complement the BUF's more tangible economic and political proposals. Both Mosley and his biographer considered fascism to be the purest expression of the war generation and its hopes. The Blackshirts aimed to 're-create that alternative society previously incarnated in the trenches and use that as a base for the political conquest of England'.[44] Inevitably, it would be left to Mosley and the fascists to 'cleanse the temple' and end a post-war era characterized by a sense of betrayal. Chesterton was certain that fascism would succeed in this precisely because it had the 'fiery force of a new religion'[45] and was grounded in the experience and sacred example of the war generation:

> Mosley and the other leaders of the modern movement have seen something of the real sublimity of mankind and it is the knowledge that this capacity for superb and selfless achievement

41. *The Fascist Week*, 21 December 1934.
42. Chesterton, *Portrait*, p. 119.
43. Chesterton, *Portrait*, p. 120.
44. Skidelsky, *Mosley*, p. 291.
45. Chesterton, *Portrait*, p. 161.

> is available for the constructive tasks of peace which is at once the spiritual basis and the inspiration of Fascism.[46]

Within a few months of producing his eulogy, Chesterton had resigned from the movement. He came to regret writing *Portrait of a Leader* and his autobiography makes no reference to his time with the BUF. Shortly after leaving in 1938, Chesterton explained his motives in a pamphlet entitled *Why I Left Mosley*.[47] Ironically, Mosley and the fascist leadership were now condemned as being as spiritually barren and as corrupt as the politicians and institutions of the hated parliamentary system. Chesterton feared that the BUF's electoral needs were swamping its principles, forcing it to act as a liberal-democratic party by sacrificing integrity for votes. He believed that the movement's noble aims were being perverted by an increasingly powerful bureaucratic clique, led by the director-general Francis-Hawkins, which regarded the BUF as an end in itself, thereby echoing the fraudulent party game. For Chesterton, Mosley had contributed to this situation by favouring party administrators at the expense of the ideals of the movement. These cronies had insulated Mosley from the realistic self-analysis and intellectual searching which was needed to advance the revolutionary creed of national socialism. Furthermore, by constantly supporting his favourites with weak arguments, the Blackshirt leader was no longer able to claim that he possessed a judicial attitude and a higher morality:

> The public aspect of this shows itself in Mosley's...refusal to deal objectively with the Movement's fortunes. 'Flops' are written up as triumphs and enormous pains are taken to titivate reports so as to give the impression of strength where there is weakness, of growth where there is declining influence...[48]

Chesterton also accused the head of the British Union of acting irresponsibly in dispensing with the services of those dedicated to the fascist faith, such as William Joyce and John Beckett. The result was that Mosley had reduced the BUF to an extension of

46. Chesterton, *Portrait*, p. 157.

47. A.K. Chesterton, *Why I Left Mosley* (London, 1938), PRO, HO 144/21247/97-101.

48. Chesterton, *Why I Left Mosley*, HO 144/21247/99.

his own ego. Having canonized his leader, Chesterton, the 'true believer', now saw him turn from saviour to false prophet. Mosley, the fascist 'god', had failed.

# Anglican Biography Since the Second World War: A Modern Tradition and its Limitations

*Garth Turner*

Charles Smyth, reviewing David Edwards's *Leaders of the Church of England 1828–1944*, wrote, 'to be deprecated is the author's recurrent and slightly irritating interest in "public school vice" and "flogging": one of the longer footnotes contains a sentence which, in its context, is both superfluous and irrelevant, and might, in charity, have been omitted'.[1]

Not to be driven back to Edwards's footnotes by so cryptic a rebuke would be not quite human. The only footnote to which it can refer occurs in his essay on Tait, where, to a passing mention of C.J. Vaughan, is appended a footnote which, beginning with his success as headmaster of Harrow, goes on: 'But in 1859 he was compelled to resign when a letter arising from an infatuation with a boy became known, and four years later he had to refuse the Bishopric of Rochester when threatened with exposure.'[2]

Whether the footnote was lacking in charity is questionable: it contained nothing new, owning its dependence on Phyllis Grosskurth's *John Addington Symonds* published some years earlier. Whether charity is a primary duty of the biographer is also questionable. Whether, in the case of Vaughan, the information was in its context superfluous and irrelevant or not, it is certainly pertinent to the study of Vaughan—a figure of interest

1. *Theology* 75 (March 1972), p. 152.
2. David Edwards, *Leaders of the Church of England 1828–1944* (Oxford: Oxford University Press, 1971), p. 105, n. 26.

in the study of the Victorian and more recent church[3]—for the incident continued to dog him. Edwards—charitably, perhaps—simplifies when he writes 'he had to refuse the Bishopric of Rochester when threatened with exposure'. He had in fact to make a humiliating withdrawal a week after accepting it and 'two resignations within four years sent tongues buzzing that there was something sinister afoot'.[4] To Dr Symonds, Vaughan's tormentor, the Mastership of the Temple, which Vaughan accepted in 1869, evidently did not transgress the stipulation that he should never accept any important ecclesiastical office. By 1879, when Vaughan became Dean of Llandaff, Symonds was dead.

The case of Vaughan, and Edwards's footnote and Smyth's rebuke, prompt a question about the canons of Anglican biography. It seems to be a defect of the biographies of many leading Anglicans that, even when written by reputable historians, they have tended to ignore the influence of personal characteristics and of domestic circumstances on the public lives of their subjects. In this they have fallen below the standard set in secular biography, especially, but not exclusively, since the Second World War, and by secular biographers writing on churchmen.

Smyth himself conformed exemplarily to the standards suggested by his professed irritation with Edwards's book. His life of Cyril Forster Garbett[5] is in many ways distinguished and, to a degree, candid: he writes of Garbett as 'shy, intimidating, austere and humourless', 'naturally highly strung...living on his nerves...a perfectionist...liable to be quite unreasonably provoked if any detail was not exactly as it ought to be'. He quotes

3. As recently as 1961 a selection from his writings was published, entitled *The Word of Life* edited and introduced by R.R. Williams, then Bishop of Leicester. Williams wrote 'for many years yet to come [Vaughan would] hold his place as a preacher's preacher'.

4. Phyllis Grosskurth, *John Addington Symonds: A Biography* (London: Longmans, 1964). The sentence quoted is on p. 37. The incident is fully recounted in ch. 11. Williams (*The Word of Life*) had written, 'he accepted [the Bishopric of Rochester] but wrote next day withdrawing, feeling that acceptance would involve too great a struggle with ambition'.

5. Charles Smyth, *Cyril Forster Garbett Archbishop of York* (London: Hodder and Stoughton, 1959).

a former curate: 'Impatience, irritability, even temper... prevailed... In the vestry once he screwed up a piece of waste paper and threw it in my face in anger, because I had made what I thought was a pardonable error in interpreting an order.'[6]

What Smyth calls 'the only trace of snobbery' in Garbett's composition is also faced fairly:

> as an Oxford undergraduate—when such things counted rather more than they do now—he had suffered from a sense of social inferiority because he had not been to a public school; which explains why during his Portsea days he had shown no interest in Portsmouth Grammar school and (so far as can be discovered) had never gone near the place.[7]

Smyth also depicts Garbett as a lonely and somewhat self-preoccupied man, facing the isolation and solitariness of celibate old age with reluctance. There are some inconclusive paragraphs of speculation as to why he never married, but it is here that Smyth shies away from the detail which might take us further into the character of this lonely man: 'there are grounds for believing that when he was Vicar of Portsea he offered his hand in marriage' he writes, but 'the circumstances are naturally obscure and private'.[8]

Recurring throughout the book are Garbett's domestic chaplains, 'his emotional safety-valves...his confidants and his sons', Smyth writes. And then he continues:

> Inevitably this relationship provoked a certain amount of jealousy and resentment, and some of the senior clergy used to grumble about his 'blue-eyed boys'. But there is little substance in the legend that Garbett's Chaplains were all public school types, young, tall, handsome, and athletic with cultivated tastes and private means (the clerical equivalent of Ouida guardsmen): some of them did possess certain of these attributes, but no single Chaplain possessed them all...[9]

The language used here ('blue-eyed boys, young, tall, handsome') may suggest that, in spite of himself, Smyth is close to

6. Smyth, *Garbett*, pp. 477, 133-34.
7. Smyth, *Garbett*, p. 464.
8. Smyth, *Garbett*, pp. 453, cf. 459-60.
9. Smyth, *Garbett*, p. 458.

what may be the root of Garbett's tensions. Any possible key to the personality of the angular, irritable, opinionated clergyman who, though maturing into a distinguished bishop, always remained angular, irritable and opinionated, is worth trying in the lock, the more so since these are characteristics which touched his dealings with others. And this key looks promising. But the matter is never explored or, beyond this, probably innocently, suggestive vocabulary, even hinted at.

If Garbett's tensions were discharged in ordinary ways—irritability, aloofness, unremittingly hard work—Lang's were melodramatic, and his biographer, J.G. Lockhart,[10] well describes this bachelor who once, when showing a group of people round Bishopthorpe, stood beneath the lately hung portrait of himself and said 'they say in that portrait I look proud, prelatical and pompous'. A member of the group, Henson, the sharp-tongued Bishop of Durham, is said to have replied 'And may I ask Your Grace to which of these epithets Your Grace takes exception?' There are many references in the biography to Lang's sense of theatre, many comparisons of him to an actor.[11] But Lockhart also devotes a chapter to the strange, introspective retreats, which for Lang passed for holidays, when it was his habit to make frank notes on his spiritual condition. 'Much of their content [is] too private for publication', Lockhart writes, yet inescapably he makes discreet use of them, for they are essential to an understanding of Lang and 'far more revealing than is anything in his autobiographical notes'.[12]

> Here in Ballure he was bitterly conscious of this conflict of Ormuzd and Ahriman, of the ambitious, forceful, histrionic prelate and the man of prayer and penitence; conscious too that those things which counted for so much with him during eleven months of the year—to be the successor of St Wilfrid or St Augustine, to walk with kings, to be on easy terms with the famous, to stay in the houses of the great—in the cool accusing

10. J.G. Lockhart, *Cosmo Gordon Lang* (London: Hodder and Stoughton, 1949).

11. Lockhart, *Lang*, p. 290 (the Henson incident) and, e.g. pp. 202, 296 and 423 (sense of theatre).

12. Lockhart, *Lang*, p. 187.

> stillness of the Highlands all this was no more than the stuff that men hang on Christmas trees for the delight of children'.[13]

Lockhart quotes Sir William Orpen, the painter of that proud, prelatical and pompous portrait, as saying 'I see seven Archbishops. Which of them am I to paint?'[14]

Lang is a remarkably unreconciled figure. Again, the chaplains may be thought to provide the clue. His favourite was Wilfred Parker, later Bishop of Pretoria. When Parker left, he wrote of him: 'I come back [from holiday] with a broken heart. I can't bear to think of the home life at Bishopsthorpe without him.'

> You see, or rather you don't see for these are not things one ought to wear on one's sleeve—my life is really rather a lonely one. It needs, not friends—I have plenty of them: not work—I have too much of it: but just that old simple human thing—someone in daily nearness to love. The fact that, for reasons sufficient to myself, I am not, and do not propose to be married, does not make the need less.

And, after his departure, Lang wrote to him almost every week 'long, intimate, and confidential letters. To no other man did he unburden himself so completely.'[15]

Perhaps Lockhart has scattered just enough clues about the book to suggest the key. Though published ten years earlier than Smyth's, his book is arguably the more open, the less deliberately obscure, of the two. But, for all his candour about many of his subject's weaknesses, he never collects these clues, never attempts to assess the influence of this part of his subject's personality on his public life and work and leadership of the Church of England—though, in the case of Lang, courtier, delighting in the friendship of the well-placed and well-bred, theatrical, it was likely to have been considerable.

Here, then are two instances of major biographies of Anglican

13. Lockhart, *Lang*, p. 190.

14. Lockhart, *Lang*, p. 458.

15. Both quotations from Lockhart, pp. 222-23. Perhaps revealingly, Garbett fastened on this. When he read Lockhart, he wrote to one of his former chaplains, G.A. Ellison, 'It is very good, and brings out the human side. He was devoted to Wilfred Parker...and wrote to him fully and freely. He was almost as miserable over his departure as I was when you left' (Smyth, *Garbett*, p. 459).

leaders which fight shy of probing powerful, determining elements in the personalities of their subjects. And there are other books about other Anglican leaders, not so prominent but exercising considerable influence in their day. Mervyn Haigh,[16] for instance, was Archbishop Davidson's Senior Chaplain at Lambeth, where he won universal plaudits (Barry quotes Archbishop Davidson as saying in 1928 'Haigh could be Archbishop of Canterbury tomorrow'[17]) and Bishop successively of Coventry and Winchester. He was a bachelor, an intelligent man with formidable administrative skills, and an acutely critical mind. But he was a perfectionist, fastidious, and overwrought, his criticisms sometimes destructively negative. The clergy in his dioceses thought him aloof, and went in awe of him. He seems to have been among those considered for Canterbury after Temple's death, but the 'strain of critical indecision' in his mind 'might have brought the Lambeth machinery to a standstill'.[18] In fact his health broke down and he was forced into early retirement. His biographer was F.R. Barry, also intelligent, but not over-wrought, and his friend for forty years. Although Haigh clearly had within him unreconciled tensions which the book recognizes ('whatever may be the medical diagnosis I have little doubt that some of his later illnesses were at least partly psychogenic in origin')[19] it offers no insight into them. His childhood seems to have been happy, the only shadow having been a disrupted schooling which left him ill-equipped to achieve the highest honours in Greats, so that he always thought of himself as having failed at Oxford.[20] To a sensitive and intelligent man such a self perception may have been scarring, the source of a deep sense of insecurity, but Barry, who was very successful in Greats, was perhaps not well placed to enter sympathetically into this: 'it only meant that his gifts were of another kind than facility in classical Greek prose...Not all first class men are men with first classes' is his

16. F.R. Barry, *Mervyn Haigh* (London: SPCK, 1964).
17. Barry, *Haigh*, p. 190.
18. Barry, *Haigh*, p. 191.
19. Barry, *Haigh*, p. 110.
20. Barry, *Haigh*, pp. 38, 41. Haigh took second classes in Moderations and Greats.

rather bluff comment on this source of life-long sensitiveness.[21] Three years later, there was a second blow to his esteem: an unsuccessful love affair within the parish resulted in his premature removal from the curacy to which he had been ordained. It left, we are told, a 'wound...[which] was never completely healed'. Perhaps here too there is a clue, but Barry refuses to discuss it: 'even now [it] must be treated with great reticence'.[22]

Of a different sort was Edward Sydney Woods. He and his wife Clemence were born into the Evangelical purple, and their collective pedigree was a roll-call of Barclays, Buxtons, Frys, Gurneys and Hoares.[23] He had done good work as Vicar of Holy Trinity, Cambridge, leaving it 'more full of life than it had been since the days of the Great Charles Simeon'.[24] During his years there he had become an increasingly liberal Evangelical, a change most revealingly illustrated by his guiding of his own sons, as they prepared for ordination, not into his own footsteps at the Evangelical Ridley Hall but to the central church Westcott House.[25] Although his, self-confessed, intellectual limitations were considerable, with his growing liberalism went imagination enough to identify with currents then running strongly (Life and Liberty, the ecumenical movement, the Student Christian Movement) and to be something of a pioneer in religious broadcasting. He was helped by a fine voice and what obituarists sometimes call a commanding presence. And he had a winning attractiveness of manner.[26] Perhaps the progression of such a one to high office was predictable, but as a

21. Barry, *Haigh*, p. 38.

22. Barry, *Haigh*, p. 41.

23. Oliver Tomkins, *The Life of Edward Woods* (London: SCM Press, 1959). On their pedigrees, pp. 10, 26, 75.

24. Tomkins, *Woods*, p. 73.

25. Robin Woods, *An Autobiography* (London: SCM Press, 1986), p. 43; cf. Tomkins, *Woods*, pp. 64f.

26. See Tomkins, *Woods*: on Life and Liberty, especially pp. 61ff.; Woods's limitations p. 61, ecumenism ch. 6, SCM, p. 103, broadcasting p. 135. On this last, cf. *Edward Sidney Woods, 94th Bishop of Lichfield. Some appreciations*, collected by Janet Stone (London: Gollancz, 1954), pp. 32f., 40 (henceforward Stone, *ESW*). His voice Tomkins, *Woods*, p. 84, his winningness, Stone, *ESW*, pp. 59ff.; see also Janet Stone, *Thinking Faces: Photographs 1953–1979* (London: Chatto and Windus, 1988), p. 11.

diocesan bishop (of Lichfield, 1937–1953) Woods's limitations were exposed.

Those whom he knew best in his sprawling midland diocese were the county grandees with whom he enjoyed days spent shooting. Early in the Lichfield years he sent his children a circular letter:

> It is evidently getting all round the Diocese that I shoot and I don't think in future I shall have much difficulty in getting as much shooting as I can spare time for. The laity seem highly delighted that the new Bishop is a sportsman. It really is a useful point of contact, as practically all the well-to-do county laity hunt and/or shoot...

In his private diary he wrote

> I enjoy enormously my very easy and natural contacts with men and women I meet at shoots and on lots of social occasions...I never have been afraid of being called a 'sport'—rather enjoyed it...but I must keep an eye open to the danger—especially the danger of passively acquiescing in their spiritual and moral standards...
>
> I have thought to myself (quite honestly) that my main motive in these contacts is evangelistic: to win them to God—but it's too easy to let this motive get rather overlaid by the mere pleasure of friendly intercourse...Moreover I don't seem to get on quick enough with the winning.[27]

There are other references in Tomkins's book to Woods's love of sport, and he prints a picture of him, gun under arm, in tweed jacket and breeches, looking the very model of a country gentleman. He writes of his increasing identification with the attitudes of the gentry: 'As the years went on, his views became more coloured by theirs, so that his reflections on political and economic matters tend to mirror the outlook of senior politicians, land-owning and industrial magnates.'[28] Woods himself ('...the mere pleasure of friendly intercourse...I don't seem to get on quick enough with the winning') almost invites a critical appraisal. But beyond the bland ('he was not blind to the dangers of being merely "a good sport"') and the defensive ('He never had anything approaching William Temple's capacity

27. Quotations from Tomkins, *Woods*, pp. 119-20.
28. Tomkins, *Woods*, p. 133.

for independent judgment, but he did often find himself in company where he stoutly defended that Archbishop's utterances and where he had to remind his hearers that "England was not made up of their sort alone"'),[29] Tomkins nowhere discusses the appropriateness of this kind of leadership of a diocese with large rural areas, certainly, where the bishop's identification with one class would be understood by most classes, but a diocese also containing the Potteries and a large part of the Black Country.

Nor is this all. Tomkins writes of Woods devolving upon his lieutenants (suffragan bishops and archdeacons) most of the administration of the diocese 'for aspects of it were irksome to him'. Soon after arriving, Woods himself wrote to his children 'however strenuous and responsible this diocesan job is and may become, I am still rejoicing in that blessed freedom from the details, toils and cares of a parish', and a little later 'I am not overpushed and overpressed, I dislike the idea, and do my best to combat it, that bishops are such frightfully pressed people that they never have time to do anything or see anyone'. This letter continues '...partly owing to the magnificent help of Bishop Hammond and Archdeacon Hodgson, who are in here every day, I can shovel a great deal of the administrative work onto their broad shoulders'. Tomkins adds

> But others, perhaps, might feel that their particular problem was one which their bishop *ought* to have handled. There were some nettles which he simply refused to grasp. Every human mind is ingenious to find self-convincing reasons for not being stung.[30]

This is really to deal very gently with his limitations: his indifference to the detail of running a large diocese, his absences, on travels or London activities, his preference for country life, his tendency to conceal his complacency in a cloud of vague pietism.

At least one of those lieutenants was blunter. After eighteen months with Woods's successor, Percy Hartill, the very able and hardworking Archdeacon of Stoke on Trent, said: 'I have had more conversation with the bishop on real pastoral matters in the last 18 months than was possible with Edward Woods in

29. Tomkins, *Woods*, pp. 119, 133.
30. Quotations from Tomkins, *Woods*, pp. 119, 120-21, 121.

sixteen years.'[31] In Ashley's memoir of Hartill, a catalogue of Woods's limitations concludes with the words 'the general total effect was of a rather restless mobility', the diocesan administration acquiring what smoothness it had 'because it relied less on its Diocesan Bishop than on "that completely dependable firm of Hammond, Hodson and Hartill".'[32] Some of the evidence for this may be inferred from Tomkins's book, but it is never explored, and it is perhaps revealing that neither his text, nor his acknowledgments suggest any indebtedness to these diocesan officers.[33]

During these years, Woods carried a private burden which must have distracted his attention even from the midland grandees to whom he was so attracted. He was devoted to his wife and family, and his marriage and family life were in many ways very happy. But his wife, always a little dotty, became increasingly, and finally disturbingly, eccentric. Tomkins writes of her 'utter lack of method' during the years at Croydon (1927–1937):

> her health, both physical and nervous, [was] often over strained. The absent-mindedness which, in good health, was merely an endearing weakness, in times of strain became both embarrassing and irritating, and in later years was to become so again.

Tomkins writes of the early years at Lichfield as a kind of remission in a growing feebleness: 'in the early days at Lichfield she reigned joyfully over her large, if slightly chaotic, domain.'[34] This is a questionable judgment, and the evidence, perhaps surprisingly, is supplied by her children.

Frank, who became Bishop of Middleton in the diocese of Manchester in 1952, and later Archbishop of Melbourne, in a memoir published soon after the deaths of his parents, wrote not only of her sad closing years when 'she could hardly bear him out of her sight, and, if he went to Town, as in some cases he was bound to do without her, she might and did pursue him

31. From A.M.D. Ashley, *Joyful Servant, The Ministry of Percy Hartill* (Abingdon, Berkshire: The Abbey Press, 1967), p. 52.

32. Ashley, *Hartill*, p. 51, n. 31.

33. It should in fairness be added that Hammond did contribute to Stone, *ESW*, pp. 50ff.

34. Tomkins, *Woods*, pp. 77, 116.

by the next train', but also of the evidently long years when 'she would announce at the breakfast table that the butter and the cream and the special marmalade were for Far [her pet name for him] and for him only'. It was, adds Frank Woods, 'a great embarrassment to him, an annoyance for the mothers of grandchildren' and, he continues, with what seems to the outsider a doubtful optimism, 'an amusement for the guests'. As her decline accelerated, Frank Woods tells of his father 'though exasperated at times to breaking point' patiently indulging her every whim. 'Some will think that his faith was in this better and more nobly demonstrated than in all his more spectacular gifts', this son adds, with a realism far exceeding that of Tomkins's discreet phrases.[35]

Their daughter, Janet, is also more explicit. Tomkins had written of Clemence Woods's 'unrepentant inability to understand the mind of her own sex', which 'made it harder for the three girls to find happiness at home'.[36] Janet Stone has in recent years told of an austere childhood, without films or plays or pantomimes, and of the impact of what Tomkins calls Clemence's endearing weakness of forgetfulness; 'my mother, being extra vague, never answered invitations for us to go to parties'; she recalls, too, being terrified of her mother's 'shocking temper'.[37]

In 1937, when she and Reynolds Stone were thinking of marrying, Janet Woods took him to Lichfield to meet her parents—'it was the first time Reynolds had ever met my parents—I'd kept him away from Mama, in particular' she adds, revealingly. A conversation between Stone and the bishop is worth recalling:

> My father said, 'Well, Reynolds Stone, can you support a wife?'
> 'I don't know', Reynolds said. 'I've been earning nearly £700 a year.'
> 'Oh, that's more than enough', said Papa. Then he said, 'Look, can you row'?

35. Stone, *ESW*, p. 119. The nearest Tomkins gets is on p. 139, perhaps discreetly echoing Frank Woods as quoted here.

36. Tomkins, *Woods*, p. 77.

37. From Stone, *Thinking Faces*, pp. 10-11. Quotations are from the Introduction described as Janet Stone in conversation with Jonathan Gili (p. 19).

> 'Yes', said Reynolds, 'I rowed for my college'.
> 'Oh well, that's absolutely splendid', said Papa, 'there's just one other question: Is there any insanity in the family'?
> 'None',
> 'Right', said Papa, 'That's fine'. And my mother said, 'Oh well, let's all have some Horlicks'.[38]

The question about insanity, one fears, may have been grounded in an anxiety very real to Woods. Certainly it is clear that, right from the start, his Lichfield episcopate was clouded by worries about an eccentric and embarrassing and increasingly demanding wife.[39] But Tomkins's narrative little considers the effect of this on Woods's episcopate.

A slight memoir of an ordinary diocesan bishop of the 1940s may not merit so critical an examination. But such memoirs become the material of the historian, and this one led Adrian Hastings, in his deservedly popular and widely read *A History of English Christianity 1920–1985* to write of Woods:

> We are still very close to the old-fashioned heart of Anglicanism, where upper class and clerical mores had quietly gelled into a single whole. Edward Woods was a priest and a gentleman. He was, everyone stressed, very 'lovable'. Yet he was a forward looking bishop who had become increasingly ecumenical and had taken a very active part in Faith and Order. He fitted the fifties very well. There was not too much wrong here.[40]

A footnote acknowledges his debt to Tomkins, on whose work his assessment of Woods is plainly based. The effectiveness of this kind of leadership is again unquestioned.

Lang, Garbett, Haigh, Woods. Four men with, in their personalities or their circumstances, ingredients which cannot have

38. Stone, *Thinking Faces*, pp. 15-16. She ends her account of this incident: 'There certainly wasn't anything like sherry in the house, let alone champagne—hard to believe now, looking back.'

39. Janet Stone provides other instances of her mother's oddness in dealing with visitors to the Palace; Stone, *Thinking Faces*, p. 18.

40. Adrian Hastings, *A History of English Christianity 1920–1985* (London: Collins, 1986, paperback 1987). That 'He fitted the fifties well' is a strange opinion on one who survived only two full years of them (d. 11 January 1953)—unless it be an obliquely devastating judgment on the Anglican leadership in that decade. Hastings is (1995) working on a biography of Oliver Tomkins.

failed to shape—perhaps profoundly—their public personalities and the way they did their work. All of them have been the subjects of biographies which have, sometimes perhaps inadvertently, hinted at the existence of these ingredients, but none has explored them deeply, still less has attempted to assess them as integral to and powerfully formative of the life of its subject.

Reasons for this are numerous. Some have been commissioned by surviving relations; some are at least constrained by the survival of relations; some are the work of friends or admirers too close to be detached. Some were published at a time when public discussion of certain characteristics could only be conducted very discreetly. Only one is not the work of a cleric, and the clerics are all of a seniority which makes it unlikely that they would not place a high premium on the public image of the Church of England.[41] This is probably true even of Smyth, the only professional academic among these writers—but also a Canon of Westminster for the ten years before he began work on Garbett.[42] It is probably substantially true also of Lang's biographer. John Gilbert Lockhart, the only layman to write the official life of a senior Anglican churchman since A.C. Benson wrote on his father in 1899, was a devout high churchman, presumably invited on the strength of his life of the Anglo-Catholic

41. Barry, Bishop of Southwell 1941–1963; Tomkins, Bristol 1959–1975. Arguably too much episcopal biography is confined within an episcopal circle: to those considered may be added (for all its excellence) Bell (Chichester 1929–1958) on Davidson; and West (Taunton 1962–1977) on Barry. If Deans and Canons are included, Ronald Jasper (Canon of Westminster and Dean of York) on Headlam and Bell, and Carpenter (Canon and Dean of Westminster) on Fisher must be added. Only Edwards, though Canon of Westminster and Dean of Norwich and Provost of Southwark, in *Leaders of the Church of England*, managed to write as though from outside the tradition.

42. His Westminster Canonry may not have exhausted Smyth's ecclesiastical ambitions: 'Smyth challenged nearly everyone and nearly everyone responded. As a consequence he received no substantial advancement in the Church of England after...Westminster.' (Maurice Cowling, *Religion and Public Doctrine in Modern England* [Cambridge: Cambridge University Press, 1980], p. 90). In 1965 he became a non-residentiary Canon of Lincoln. One who knew him at the time has told me of his delight which was quite disproportionate to the modest nature of the honour.

leader, the second Viscount Halifax (1839–1934)—a useful, but notably uncritical, biography.[43]

But there is another tradition. In modern Anglican biography it begins with Sir Geoffrey Faber's contribution to the celebration of the centenary of the Oxford movement in 1933. In *Oxford Apostles* he placed his great-uncle, Frederic William Faber, together with others of the Oxford fathers—John Henry Newman and Richard Hurrell Froude, more particularly—on the psychiatrist's couch. Faber's honesty in detecting a root of homosexuality especially in Faber and Newman and Froude caused some scandal at the time, and the book did not escape criticism.[44] But it is noteworthy that, although on a subject remote, one supposes, from popular interest, it was in print more or less continuously for nearly sixty years. Faber's attempt 'to grasp the working of his grandfather's mind' apparently continues to appeal to many other minds. Even though the detail of his speculations may be open to challenge, Faber's intention, his attempt to relate the personal condition of his subjects to their public lives, has a realism from which other writers of ecclesiastical biography could learn.[45]

The only archbishop of Canterbury to have undergone comparable treatment is Edward White Benson. Once more, Edwards's short study is replete with accounts of public school severity ('he ruled through terror') and 'vaguely Freudian' guesses of the kind that so affronted Smyth, as well as of the depressive and histrionic elements in his subject.[46] But, once

43. For Lockhart's Anglo-Catholicism, see *The Times*, 9 January 1960 (death announcement): Requiem and funeral to be at St Matthew's Westminster (a noted Anglo-Catholic Church); 15 January 1960 (obituary): 'for a considerable time he was closely associated with the Church Union.' On his *Viscount Halifax* cf. The Earl of Birkenhead, *The Life of Lord Halifax* (London: Hamish Hamilton, 1965), on the second Viscount, '...even his biographer, Lockhart, who has little critical to say of him...' (p. 20).

44. Geoffrey Faber, *Oxford Apostles. A Character Study of the Oxford Movement*. For an assessment see Piers Brendon, *Hurrell Froude and the Oxford Movement* (Paul Elek, 1974), pp. 60ff. and notes.

45. Faber's book, with its psycho-sexual analysis, is very much a book of its period. At about the same time, Elsie Harrison made a similar start on Wesley in *Son to Susanna* (1937).

46. Edwards, *Leaders*, ch. 6, especially pp. 194, 196, 203ff.

more, Edwards is only the first *clerical* historian to write openly about these aspects of his subject, and to assess their effect on his public life; a footnote reveals his dependence on David Newsome's *A History of Wellington College 1859–1959*, in which the picture of Benson had included his uncontrollable temper, his austere school discipline, his imperious manner and temperament, the streak of the histrionic in him.[47] Benson has been the subject of two more studies which carry this kind of analysis further, lingering on his manic-depressive temperament, his marriage (there is a suggestion that his wife Mary was lesbian), and speculating on the effect these parents had on their gifted but strange children.[48] It is doubtless an interest in these children, especially Arthur Christopher, sentimental essayist and author of 'Land of Hope and Glory', and Edward Frederick, popular novelist, that has sustained curiosity about Benson. But the result is that Benson, unlikely in anyone's estimate to be the greatest nineteenth-century Archbishop of Canterbury, is the best understood; his character, so far as may be a century later, is laid bare.

Which brings us, by an odd route, to Michael Ramsey. Owen Chadwick's life of Ramsey was so successful that it was quickly reprinted.[49] The book is almost a history of the Church of England for Ramsey's years at Canterbury (1961–1974); Chadwick's thematic chapters on those years cover the wide range of issues—national and international, social and political, Anglican and ecumenical, theological and ecclesiastical—with which the Church of England, and so Ramsey, was confronted. But there are aspects of its subject's character which the book does not face, and so necessarily fails to integrate with the public life it portrays with such authority.

First and foremost, Ramsey was a theologian and a scholar, a thing he never forgot, nor does Chadwick; there are many

47. David Newsome, *A History of Wellington College 1859–1959* (John Murray, 1959). For these characteristics, see pp. 174, 89, 90.

48. Betty Askwith, *Two Victorian Families* (Chatto and Windus, 1971); David Williams, *Genesis and Exodus: A portrait of the Benson Family* (London: Hamish Hamilton, 1979).

49. Owen Chadwick, *Michael Ramsey. A Life* (Oxford: Oxford University Press, 1990).

references scattered through the book to his scholarly and theological approach to the issues that faced him: 'He knew he was an academic and student of the New Testament, and that this is what he could contribute'.[50] His first book, *The Gospel and the Catholic Church*, was published in 1936: 'it was seen to be an original contribution of power, and that a new force in Christian thinking had appeared among the Churches of England' Chadwick writes.[51] And it would be hard to exaggerate its significance for Ramsey: with it, he sprang into the view of the interested public and it is arguable that nothing he wrote later was its equal.[52] But Chadwick's paragraphs on the book give little idea of the thought in which its power lay, nor does he attend seriously to the content of the later books.[53] Yet Ramsey made his name as a theological writer; he was raised to the episcopate expressly as a scholar-bishop in the Durham tradition, of which he was very conscious, preaching on it, and specially on Westcott, at his enthronement there.[54] Ramsey's learning and his theological stance, how they developed, how they changed, their limitations, is a theme that runs through his life and ought to run through the book. Within parentheses and in passing Chadwick writes: 'Notice the change which the Durham professorship, and Joan's coming, wrought—in 1940 no one could conceive of this absent-minded man as a bishop.'[55] He is surely right, especially about Ramsey's marriage. The transformation of the bachelor whose pupils at Lincoln thought him too odd for eminence; whose fellow curates at Boston thought him strange for whistling in processions, but 'took it for granted that this was Ramsey'; who, when Vicar of St Benet's, went about Cambridge in trousers so threadbare that his underwear was visible; whose churchwarden was relieved at his departure, so

50. Chadwick, *Ramsey*, p. 113.

51. Chadwick, *Ramsey*, p. 49.

52. Cf. Macquarrie, 'I am inclined to say that this first book was possibly also his best'. Quoted by Michael De-la-Noy, *Michael Ramsey. A Portrait* (London: Collins, 1990), p. 91.

53. E.g. the purely factual list of the main writings of the Durham professorship, p. 63.

54. Michael Ramsey, *Durham Essays and Addresses* (London: SPCK, 1956), pp. 87ff. Chadwick, *Ramsey*, p. 72.

55. Chadwick, *Ramsey*, p. 72.

embarrassing was he; whose new colleagues at Durham found him so eccentric that one, seeing him walking down the Bailey with one foot in the gutter and the other on the pavement, pronounced him a lunatic—[56] the transformation of this bachelor into one who was *episcopabile* must be the work of the woman whom he married in 1942. Although a tribute to Joan Ramsey's influence follows the account of the wedding,[57] there is little attempt to trace it through the years of her husband's episcopate. But it must have contributed to his ecclesiastical eminence. Here, then, is a second theme, inseparable from Ramsey's personality, which, one surmises, would help the reader to understand him and his success, if it had been followed through in the book.

Chadwick treats Ramsey's eccentricity as an amusing characteristic, but little more. He never pauses to consider what its effects may have been. He remarks on his low boredom threshold, doodling (often writing out the succession lists at Canterbury or 10 Downing Street) when chairman of meetings, even of the British Council of Churches or the Lambeth Conference, so that an aide would need to brief him at the end of a speech before the meeting could continue; on his imperfect administration; on his hopelessness at personnel-management.[58] Nowhere, though, does he consider these as limitations, preferring to treat them with good-natured indulgence, part of his subject's eccentricity—and, as any reader of his books knows, Chadwick loves stories about eccentrics.

Chadwick is arguably too close to Ramsey to be more critical than this: they were close friends; Ramsey himself commissioned the book, he was a frequent visitor to Selwyn as the guest of Chadwick, who was with him the day before he died; Ramsey 'would assume that his close scholarly friends like the Chadwicks or Christopher Evans were run of the mill'.[59]

But Chadwick's was not the only book about Ramsey to have been published in 1990; there is also *Michael Ramsey, A Portrait*, by Michael De-la-Noy, Ramsey's press officer from 1967 to 1970.

56. Chadwick, *Ramsey*, pp. 45-46, 53, 55, 57.
57. Chadwick, *Ramsey*, p. 59.
58. Chadwick, *Ramsey*, pp. 113, 117, 275.
59. Chadwick, *Ramsey*, p. v, De-la-Noy, *Portrait*, pp. 235, 242.

Dismissed after an error of judgment, he quickly published the curiously titled *A Day in the Life of God*, a bitter book about the Church of England, and one very critical of Ramsey. His later book is mellower, and appreciative of its subject's qualities and achievements. But it is a useful supplement to Chadwick, and, sometimes, a corrective to his judgments. The differences between the two books are suggestive.

Chadwick for instance draws a picture of Ramsey's management of his staff which recognizes the existence of blemishes: 'He was curiously bad, at times, with his staff' he writes. A friend is quoted as saying he was 'hopeless at man-management' and two 'witnesses' 'even use the word "callous" to describe the impression he sometimes gave of ingratitude towards the staff'. Chadwick defends him, saying 'it was hard for them to realize he did not think words important in personal relationships. He assumed that they knew him to be grateful...'[60] Following Harold Macmillan, he depicts Ramsey as 'Mary', and, passing over his difficulties very lightly, says he was finally rescued from the 'Martha-chores' by the appointment of an episcopal chaplain because 'a priest chaplain was not senior enough to cope with the problems of the other bishops'.[61] De-la-Noy (who saw from the inside) is more severe; his book provides a picture of Ramsey's management and administration bordering on the chaotic. His dealings with the suffragan bishops who helped him in the diocese of Canterbury are described as 'at times little less than a disgrace'. One of them, Hughes of Croydon, for instance, was both a director of ordinands in the diocese and Bishop to the Forces. He found that each of his groups of charges—the ordinands, and the service chaplains—was invited to Lambeth Palace, and he was not. He would learn of appointments to parishes in Croydon from the newspapers.[62] It was the same with the staff at Lambeth Palace:

> The idea of a weekly staff meeting at Lambeth Palace attended by members of his household would have been anathema to him, and communication between the various departments was

60. Chadwick, *Ramsey*, p. 117.
61. Chadwick, *Ramsey*, pp. 115, 118.
62. De-la-Noy, *Portrait*, p. 163.

conducted on an *ad hoc* basis. Inevitably, in the heat of the moment some crucial decision would fail to be shared.[63]

De-la-Noy represents the appointment of the Martha bishop as the way out of a situation resented, he says, by the other bishops—the excessive influence of a young domestic chaplain. (Chadwick had written 'a priest-chaplain was not senior enough...'; no one recalling Bell or Haigh will endorse that *tout court.*) Of this solution, De-la-Noy writes 'while Tiarks got on all right with the other bishops, he was virtually ignored by Michael Ramsey... In the event, they had little in common...Tiarks was soon expressing distress, because the Archbishop never consulted him...'[64] There are other instances of a difference in emphasis between the descriptions of administration in the two books where it is difficult to resist the impression that Chadwick indulges or glosses over defects which De-la-Noy describes faithfully.[65]

De-la-Noy also seems to do greater justice to Joan Ramsey. He quotes Hughes on her role when they visited the clergy: 'what he would have done when visiting the vicarages without Joan, I can't think. People liked her very much indeed'. (Ramsey was notoriously silent, almost completely without small talk.) De-la-Noy writes of her: 'she more or less made sure he was properly dressed, although on one occasion in Newcastle he very nearly appeared on television with a cleaner's tag attached to his suit... The debt he owed to her management of Lambeth and Canterbury...cannot be exaggerated.'[66] Other aspects of Ramsey's personality are also depicted, it seems realistically, by De-la-Noy. He acquired pastoral responsibilities. Chadwick documents for instance his growing reputation as a confessor: at Lincoln 'some of the students started to use him as their confessor'; at Boston 'he was in demand as a confessor' and 'he knew that many souls valued him for this work'; at St Benet's,

63. De-la-Noy, *Portrait*, p. 214.

64. De-la-Noy, *Portrait*, pp. 211-12.

65. E.g. the way the post was handled: Chadwick, *Ramsey*, p. 117, De-la-Noy, *Portrait*, p. 214.

66. De-la-Noy, *Portrait*, pp. 163. 217-18. Joan Ramsey died in 1995. Her obituary in the *Guardian* (14 February 1995) was, appropriately, written by Michael De-la-Noy.

Cambridge, he 'had a time announced for hearing confessions and some people came'; at Durham 'he was in demand for the hearing of confessions'. Back in Cambridge 'he was in demand for preaching and conducting retreats'.[67]

De-la-Noy confirms this picture of Ramsey the pastor, describing two incidents from the archiepiscopate when, though engaged with others, he broke off in order to bless individuals who approached him, and one of him, when travelling in a taxi, taking pains to set at ease the driver, a former priest whom he had ordained.[68] But he tells also of pastoral ineptness. Much in his dealings with his staff, as De-la-Noy reports them, might be so described: 'his seeming lack of concern for those who served him, even though he knew they loved him, was one of the hallmarks of life at Lambeth Palace.' A chaplain is quoted as saying 'I could be swinging from the bannisters one morning, and the Archbishop would never notice'. And De-la-Noy recounts an incident in Jamaica when a police motorcyclist escorting his car was injured; Ramsey sat frozen in his car, rather than getting out to offer comfort. De-la-Noy speculates about 'a deep fear of emotional commitment. His feelings about the pain and unhappiness of other people were something he almost found impossible to express.' He tells the strange story also of Ramsey, a Durham Professor aged thirty-seven, needing before his marriage to seek basic sexual instruction from his sister, a general practitioner—a remarkable lacuna, it seems, in one whose pastoral reputation, at least as a confessor, was so high.[69] To Chadwick's picture of Ramsey—devout, scholarly, unworldly, eccentric, amusing—De-la-Noy adds darker hues.

Lastly, De-la-Noy has tried to assess the theological writings of this pre-eminently theological archbishop, providing here also a corrective to the seeming disinclination of Chadwick to do so. Not himself equipped for the task, he has consulted a number of theologians—including Don Cupitt, Leslie Houlden, David Jenkins, John Macquarrie, and Harry Williams—who expound Ramsey's thought, and offer critical assessments of it. The result is a series of disjointed comments, but the comments

67. Chadwick, *Ramsey*, pp. 45, 52, 55, 59, 70.

68. De-la-Noy, *Portrait*, pp. 161, 167.

69. De-la-Noy, *Portrait*, pp. 220, 114.

are not without interest, and the book at least attempts to 'place' Ramsey as a theologian in a way that Chadwick does not. De-la-Noy, a former journalist, has written a number of secular biographical sketches. His book does not have the authority of Chadwick's. But once again, the secular writer, outside the distinctively Anglican tradition, reverent and discreet, sketched in this essay,[70] has added detail which roots firmly in the frailty of human life a churchman in danger of being wafted prematurely heavenwards.

70. Only sketched: it lacks, for instance, any discussion of Jasper's two fine studies (though within the tradition sketched here) of Headlam and Bell or Chadwick on Hensley Henson, or Iremonger on Temple, or Carpenter on Fisher.